TEACHING
PUBLIC SPEAKING
ONLINE
with
THE ART OF
PUBLIC SPEAKING
Eighth Edition
by
STEPHEN E. LUCAS

JENNIFER COCHRANE
Indiana University—Purdue University at Indianapolis

Boston   Burr Ridge, IL   Dubuque, IA   Madison, WI   New York   San Francisco   St. Louis
Bangkok   Bogotá   Caracas   Kuala Lumpur   Lisbon   London   Madrid   Mexico City
Milan   Montreal   New Delhi   Santiago   Seoul   Singapore   Sydney   Taipei   Toronto

The McGraw·Hill Companies

Mc
Graw
Hill

Teaching Public Speaking Online with
THE ART OF PUBLIC SPEAKING, Eighth Edition, By Stephen E. Lucas
Jennifer Cochrane

Published by McGraw-Hill, an imprint of The McGraw-Hill Companies, Inc., 1221 Avenue of the Americas, New York, NY 10020. Copyright © 2004 by The McGraw-Hill Companies, Inc.
All rights reserved.
The contents, or parts thereof, may be reproduced in print form solely for classroom use with
THE ART OF PUBLIC SPEAKING
provided such reproductions bear copyright notice, but may not be reproduced in any other form or for any other purpose without the prior written consent of The McGraw-Hill Companies, Inc., including, but not limited to, in any network or other electronic storage or transmission, or broadcast for distance learning.

1 2 3 4 5 6 7 8 9 0 QPD/QPD 0 9 8 7 6 5 4 3

ISBN 0-07-256418-0

www.mhhe.com

About the Author

Jennifer Cochrane graduated from Sylvania High School, Sylvania, Ohio in 1966 and went on to receive a BA from Heidelberg College, Tiffin, Ohio, in 1970, majoring in secondary education, speech and Spanish. Ms. Cochrane earned an MA in Communication from Purdue University in 1972, focusing on oral interpretation and American literature.

From 1973 to 1977, Ms. Cochrane served as Director of Instructional Broadcasting for two K-12 Cooperative Educational Service Agencies: one in southern Wisconsin and the other in northwest Wisconsin. She served as Assistant Director of Continuing Education programs at the University of Wisconsin-Stout at Menomonie from 1977 to 1979.

In 1980, she was hired as associate faculty at Indiana University-Purdue University at Indianapolis (IUPUI), Department of Communication Studies, to teach the basic course in public speaking. In 1992, she redesigned and taught the Voice and Diction course and was appointed as assistant basic course director, under the supervision of Dr. B. Bruce Wagener.

Ms. Cochrane was appointed basic course director in 1998 and led the redesign of the basic course in concert with a faculty task force. She and two colleagues have written an ancillary entitled *The R110 Student Coursebook to accompany The Art of Public Speaking*, now in its sixth edition. In late 1999, she was asked to convert the basic course to a Web-based format. In spring 2001, the first online public speaking course was successfully implemented, and it continues to this day. Ms. Cochrane has edited and compiled a similar ancillary for the online course entitled *The Student Coursebook for Communication R110 Online*.

In the fall of 2003, Ms. Cochrane will assume the position of Director of Online Teaching and Learning for the Department. of Communication Studies at IUPUI.

Acknowledgments

I want to thank and acknowledge the following people for sharing their higher order thinking, expertise and encouragement with me:

- Natasha Flowers, Instructional Design Consultant, Center for Teaching and Learning, Indiana University-Purdue University at Indianapolis (IUPUI).
- Elizabeth Rubens, Instructional Design Consultant, Center for Teaching and Learning, IUPUI.
- Stephen Brunner, Design Consultant, Cyber Learning Labs, Indianapolis.
- Stephen E. Lucas, Faculty, Author, Scholar, University of Wisconsin, Madison.
- John Parrish-Sprowl, Chair, Department of Communication Studies, IUPUI.
- Kim White-Mills, Resident Faculty, Department of Communication Studies, IUPUI.
- Kristy Sheeler, Resident Faculty, Department of Communication Studies, IUPUI.
- Nanette Kauffman-Giles, Senior Sponsoring Editor, McGraw-Hill, Inc., my encouraging idea editor.
- Kassi Radomski, Freelance Development Editor, and Rhona Robbin, Director of Development and Media Technology, McGraw-Hill, Inc., my patient editors during the writing and revising process.

The following people have had the experience of using *The Art of Public Speaking* in their online public speaking courses, and took their valuable time to share their experiences with me:

- Nan Peck, Northern Virginia Community College, Annandale, Virginia.
- Linda Heil, Harford Community College, Bel Air, Maryland.
- Leslie Klipper, San Diego Community College, San Diego, California.
- Jennifer Reem, NOVA Southeastern University, Ft. Lauderdale, Florida.

Finally, I want to thank God and my family, who know that I will not be in front of a computer permanently—it only seems like it.

Preface

If you are reading this supplement, you may be an instructor who is developing a public speaking course online for the first time, or you may want to improve an online course you have already developed. Perhaps you have been asked by an administrator to create your course, or you are just doing it for the challenge. Maybe you are frustrated with your current online public speaking course and are searching for new ideas. Whatever your situation, this supplement is designed to help you create a new course or improve your current course and to expedite the time it takes to put your course in a Web-based environment.

This book is not meant to be inclusive, nor is it a "how-to" recipe book. Oral assignments are mentioned but not emphasized. Instead, the purpose of this booklet is to help you develop the *content-based* parts of your course, for that is what the Web does best. The supplement is divided into the following major areas:

- An **Introduction**, which discusses five characteristics of the typical online classroom.
- **Changing the Web Environment into a Learning Environment** looks at four key characteristics of the Web environment, and how you can develop or modify your course to accommodate those characteristics. It also explains and integrates five course design principles that go along with these characteristics.
- **The Process of Course Development** provides a step-by-step process for the development of your online course.
- A **Compendium of Online Activities** contains activities based on the Lucas text, select Lucas supplements, and additional resources, which have been adapted for an online delivery format.
- **Teaching Tips and Resources** includes tips for the online teacher, excerpts from a course schedule and syllabus, a survey for potential online learners, and a task list for project management.
- A **Suggested Readings** section, which includes related book and journal articles, and online resources for further study.

Of special note is the Compendium of Online Activities, which features activities based on the "Exercises for Critical Thinking" and "Applying the Power of Public Speaking" at the ends of the chapters in *The Art of Public Speaking*, eighth edition, full student speeches on the Lucas Student CD-ROM, and *Selections from The Speech Communication Teacher*. There are a few activities based on other sources. Every assignment is tied to a learning outcome and fulfills a Web course design principle (explained in Changing the Web Environment into a Learning Environment). They are written as models for you to use or to stimulate your own creative energies when you go about the business of designing your own online course assignments. Most of them have been "road tested" and can be used with confidence.

The activities and experiences described in this supplement are based on Web-based course development and teaching over a three-year period at Indiana University-Purdue

University at Indianapolis (IUPUI). The basic speech course, The Fundamentals of Speech Communication, which is the institution's general education requirement, was put online in the spring of 2001 and has been taught every semester since. The actual course development period lasted about one year. The goal was to create an online course that offered opportunities similar to the traditional course. The same course objectives were used for the online class as the traditional classes, making the online class fully transferable.

The Fundamentals of Speech Communication is designed as a computer-mediated, mixed mode public speaking course consisting of five speeches: one introductory, two informative, and two persuasive. Students are required to come to class on three Saturdays during the semester to present three of the five speaking assignments; the entire class must be present to hear the speeches; and they take time for oral critiques. All speeches are videotaped. The speeches are designed incrementally, with new and more sophisticated skills added on to each speech during the semester.

The IUPUI online speech course contains numerous homework assignments designed to bring students to a certain level of competency before each speech. All of the written assignments are retrieved and posted online. The assignments include readings, tests, papers, short answers to questions, forum discussions, and observations of recorded and live speakers.

The IUPUI course is entirely textbook-driven. Telecourses and streaming audio or video lectures were considered, but from a technological standpoint, the streaming video would leave out a number of students who didn't possess the right equipment. It would also cost a lot in time and expertise. Instructional designers cautioned about doing too much, so *The Art of Public Speaking*, 8th ed. is used as "teacher" for the following reasons:

1) It is an easy-to-read, "basic" book, and most students are capable of reading all of the chapters in a semester.
2) It is replete with excellent examples of rhetorical concepts.
3) The "Exercises for Critical Thinking" and "Applying the Power of Public Speaking" activities are perfect for reflective online assignments.
4) Disk Two of the Lucas CD-ROM contains full student speeches, which are an excellent way for students to "hear and see" speeches similar to what they would experience in a traditional setting.
5) Disk One of the Lucas CD-ROM contains video clips of speech excerpts, the popular interactive self-study test questions and a variety of other features.
6) The developers wanted to find out just how effective *The Art of Public Speaking* was for an online course. After all, if students can learn to be good speakers by reading what Stephen Lucas wrote and then *doing* it without an instructor's presence, that is yet another reason why it is the number one public speaking text in the nation!

Another unique aspect of the IUPUI course is an online learning survey that each potential student has to submit in order to be considered for the course. It assesses the learning style and technical expertise of each student. It is no predictor of success, but it forces students to think about how they learn, and whether online learning is the best way for them to acquire knowledge and skills in public speaking. This survey is the beginning of an initial conversation with students regarding their readiness for online learning. It is quite helpful, and many students self-select out of the course after taking the survey. A copy of this survey appears in the Teaching Tips and Resources section.

As education and business embrace computer-mediated instruction, you may wonder if it is a trend that will fade away, and whether you should bother to get involved. You may be wondering if it is even possible to generate adequate public speakers in this manner. You may have no choice in the matter. However, as scholars, we owe it to our discipline to find out.

There is one thing that you may discover. After years of enduring the "skills-based" stereotype, the basic speech course in its online format can be transformed into a "content-based" course with depth. Reflective thinking and intellectual discussions happen online, whereas there may be no time for such things in the traditional classroom. Students challenge the instructor and the content more often and ask deeper and more probing questions. Self-analyses and outside speaker evaluations tend to be more thoughtful. In short, the Web environment can foster the critical intellect of your students in new and better ways if the course is designed effectively.

Whatever the future of online instruction is, your work in online course development will make you a better teacher because you will begin to find better ways for the student to discover the information, rather than provide that information for them. You will be instrumental in helping students to "teach themselves" to learn. And that's what life-long learning is all about.

The Introduction that follows discusses the characteristics of the online classroom, so that you can draw conclusions about how the online environment differs from your traditional classroom.

Introduction

That "public speaking *online*" is a bit of an oxymoron is not lost on most people. Potential students call and ask how one takes a speech course online. Those of us who have been asked to develop a computer-mediated public speaking or hybrid speech course also have wondered how public speaking can possibly happen in a Web-based environment. How can students develop interpersonal and public speaking skills without face-to-face interaction with an audience? Isn't this a little like teaching math without numbers? It seems that the very nature of *computer-mediated instruction*, or teaching and learning via the Internet, does not fit with our discipline. It is as if the mainspring of the watch has been disconnected and we are still asked to tell the time. How can we possibly mimic online what goes on in a real communication classroom?

The answer is that we *cannot* create a traditional classroom experience online. The online teaching and learning environment is uniquely different from the traditional classroom situation with the inherent problem being the absence of the face-to-face interaction so crucial to the teaching and learning of communication skills. What we can do, however, is learn how to create an online teaching and learning environment that will *prepare* students to give their oral presentations effectively. The purpose of the subsequent discussion is to help you begin the journey from a traditional classroom mindset into an online one. The following characteristics of a typical online classroom environment should be considered neither as advantageous nor disadvantageous. Rather, consider them as descriptions of the actual Web-based learning environment that must be managed in order to turn the passive Web environment into a Web *learning* environment. These five characteristics are summarized in Figure 1 on page 7.

Characteristics of the Online Classroom

1. *Your students are physically absent.* The implications of teaching an online class extend beyond the physical absence of the students. The biggest challenge in an online environment is that there is little or no social support from other students and the teacher. This type of support is more likely in a face-to-face setting. Since learning is known to be a social endeavor, interpreted and assessed through social contexts, it is important to note that the virtual classroom does not lend itself to social interaction unless that interaction is embedded in the course design.

   Lack of human presence causes a feeling of isolation on the part of many online students. They may feel invisible. They may fail to engage with the course content. It is easy for students to feel as though they are the "only ones" with certain problems and concerns. These frustrations, compounded by the normal problem of speech anxiety, may cause a heightened feeling of "aloneness." Unless there are social bonds created between the teacher and the students, the nurturing and guiding that teachers do in their traditional public speaking classes cannot take place. Without any social interaction, students may find it difficult to encourage each other. The result of this intense psychological distance may be high attrition in the class.

2. *Your students will do most of their communicating with you by writing.* Most, if not all, of the course management information, schedule, and assignments will be retrieved from the Web. Homework assignments will be submitted on the Web, through your *courseware* platform e-mail system. (Courseware is a type of information management software—such as Web CT, Blackboard, Oncourse, Angel, and PageOut—used for online courses.) Students will communicate with you almost exclusively by e-mail. As a result, there will be more reading and writing done as a prerequisite to your speaking assignments—more perhaps, than in your traditional face-to-face setting.

Because the Web is an excellent medium by which to convey the written word, you will find that your course will contain more opportunities for students to write in-depth answers to homework assignments, and you, in turn, will be doing a lot more reading and commenting. One of the surprising consequences of this, assuming your course is well designed, is that you will know your students intellectually far better than you do in your traditional classroom. Students in an effectively designed online class tend to write more reflective answers and show remarkable abilities to apply course content. This opportunity to focus on content will be a delight to those instructors who have endured the "skills-based" labeling of their classes for so many years.

Students also tend to respond more freely in an online environment. Academically, this can be a very positive thing. Your painfully shy students who typically don't speak up in class will converse freely on the Web. Your class "participation" will be better, generally speaking, because everyone is required to participate and there is "time" for everyone to do so.

On the other hand, it is very easy for students to respond to the instructor tactlessly or negatively because the object of the students' frustrations is a faceless entity with seemingly no feelings. However, the presence of a good online social structure will tend to minimize such occurrences.

Naturally, all this communication may result in an enormous burden of reading for the instructor. Although careful planning can minimize the time spent in front of the computer, truly effective teaching takes a great deal of time in an online learning environment—perhaps more than you would expect. As the instructor, your written communication *is* your pedagogy. With the possible exception of those of you who hear and critique your student speeches face-to-face, most of the time you will be teaching through the written word. Although you can send group e-mail messages, most of your e-mails will be private ones of encouragement, evaluation, or assessment. If you have a class of twenty to thirty students or more, responding to their written assignments and wants and needs is a daunting task requiring many hours for its effective completion.

3. *Class communication is largely asynchronous.* The word *asynchronous* basically means not occurring at the same time. Your cyber classroom will not function in a single unit of time, like your traditional classroom. Students can access your course

and assignments at any time of day or night from any part of the world. The benefits of an asynchronous class lie mainly in the time allowed or taken for crafting a well-thought-out response, whether it is by the teacher who is evaluating a homework assignment, or by the student who is submitting it. The opportunity to practice writing messages that are precise and appropriate will ultimately foster an e-mail environment in which satisfying intellectual discussions can take place. This more disciplined use of e-mail is a far cry from the knee-jerk, reactive messaging usually attributed to that medium.

4. *There is a student and teacher role reversal.* One of the more fascinating phenomena in a well-designed online teaching and learning environment is a role reversal that naturally happens when the students and teachers begin to understand and use the online environment effectively.

    As the teacher, you will learn to put your pupils in the center of the learning process by creating opportunities for them to discover, build, reflect upon, share and apply information. Much of it will be the same type of information that you transferred to them in your traditional class, either by lecture, handout, or some other means. In an online class, you are more of a facilitator, guide, coach, or resource than you are a source of information. Your job will be to create an environment that guides your students to acquire and apply the information by themselves.

    Students, on the other hand, assume a great deal more responsibility for their own learning. Students "teach themselves to learn" by interacting with the academic opportunities provided, constructing and sharing information, managing their time, and using that time for critical thinking, reflection, and application.

5. *Your students depend on technology to submit most of their work and to communicate.* The key word in the previous sentence is "depend." The traditional class situation is a lot more stable than the online class because of the fallibility of technology. If an Internet service provider has problems, communication with students is disrupted, and assignments may not get submitted or graded. If your institutional Intranet hiccups or a server goes down, significant downtime may occur, disrupting a test or another exercise that is dependent on a time window. Computers crash. The power goes out. Attachments don't get attached. The list goes on. Backup plans and a flexible attitude are essential in an online learning environment, perhaps more so than in a traditional one.

    As disconcerting as technology can be, it is a method of education and communication considered "fun" by many students. The communication is convenient and fast, and students' work can be created with publication quality, color and style. Students have unlimited access to a vast array of information and use a mind-boggling variety of technical tools.

    Teachers have the same access to information and tools, which can be used strategically to provide learning opportunities for students with diverse learning styles. Tools at teachers' disposal include forum discussions; group and partnership projects and interaction; streaming audio and/or video files; and links to interactive websites.

Figure 1
Online Classroom Characteristics

Web Classroom Characteristics	Online Teacher or Student Response
1. Physical absence	1. Create online social presence
2. More written communication	2. Use communication as pedagogy
3. Asynchronous class time	3. Create reflective, intellectual responses
4. Teacher/student role reversal	4. Teacher become facilitator, guide, coach; student becomes self-teacher, responsible for own learning
5. Work dependent on technology	5. Create backup plans; use technology for learning styles; have fun

Now that you know the major characteristics of an online classroom, the next section takes an in depth look at the pedagogical transition that must be made from the traditional classroom to the Web environment, and then from a passive web learning environment to one that promotes active learning. Making this transition requires that you understand in more detail the characteristics of the Web environment and how you can make it work to produce an active learning environment for your students.

Changing the Web Environment into a Learning Environment

If we compare our traditional classroom teaching and learning situations to the Web environment, we will naturally begin to list advantages and disadvantages. While a list of this nature can be quite helpful, it can also lead us to believe that certain kinds of learning, like public speaking, may not be possible online. Merely listing advantages and disadvantages may not offer enough insight into the true nature of the online learning paradigm with regard to course and assignment design.

Instead, the approach in this section is to discuss how four key characteristics of the Web environment will impact traditional notions of teaching and learning, and how these characteristics will affect online course development and assignment design. In addition, this section will provide specific principles for online course development based on these characteristics. The integration of traditional classroom and Web environment characteristics with the Web *learning* environment characteristics, and the resultant course design principles are summarized in Figure 2. The course design principles are based on the author's experience and research in this area.

It is important to note that, while developing a course for online delivery, you are making a three-step journey into a new instructional paradigm. The first step is to understand the traditional classroom in which you (the teacher) are the primary source of information. You control the learning objectives and outcomes and manage the transfer (active or passive) of information to the students, who are the "receivers." The traditional classroom is one in which people are physically present and interact during a limited time period. Communication happens in real time and generally, there are a limited variety of classroom tools used or available during the time the class meets.

In step two, you seek to understand the nature of the Web environment itself in order to become acquainted with the new medium of instructional delivery. The passive nature of the Web; the absence of physical contact; communicating through the written word; and the huge amount of media, information and tools, are major characteristics of this delivery system. Understanding these characteristics will help you to discover the best ways to use them in the next step.

Finally, in step three, knowledge of the Web delivery system will enable you to shape and manage select Web characteristics for effective student-initiated learning. Embedding social interaction and collaboration in course assignments, providing opportunities for critical and written reflection, and utilizing a variety of media and electronic tools for learning and assessment are three ways that Web characteristics are managed to inspire the active, student-initiated learning that is the hallmark of effective computer-mediated education.

While the nature of the Web cannot be changed to accommodate our traditional classroom pedagogy, we can manage it more effectively by modifying our pedagogy so that it is strongly supported and enhanced by the characteristics of this unique delivery system.

<u>Figure 2</u>
Characteristics of the Web Environment,
the Active Learning Web Environment, and
Related Course Design Principles

Traditional Learning Environment	Web Environment	Web Learning Environment	Course Design Principles
Teacher is source of information management and transfer	Medium is passive source for informational transfer and management	Student is source of information transfer and management	#1: Use active rather than passive strategies
Physical presence and interpersonal contact	Absence of physical contact	Social interaction embedded	#2: Frequent and timely interaction with teacher #3: Embed student social interaction in assignments
Based on synchronous oral expression	Based on written words and symbols—synchronous	Promotes reflective thought	#4: Encourage critical reflection and response
Traditional classroom tools and methods	Infinite variety of media, information and tools	Tools and media used to enhance diverse learning styles	#5: Pedagogy should drive choice of technology

Four Characteristics Of The Web That Affect Teaching And Learning Online

The goal of this section is to help you identify and understand how four relevant characteristics of the Web environment will help you to develop or modify your course to fit a Web-based environment. Those four characteristics are:

1) The Web is primarily a passive medium for managing and transferring information.
2) The Web is an environment with an absence of face-to-face contact.
3) The Web is a medium based on the written word.
4) The Web is a resource that accesses a vast array of tools, information and media.

Understanding these characteristics will help you maximize the strengths of the Web and minimize the weaknesses that may seem to preclude the teaching and learning of communication skills online.

1) A Passive Medium for Managing and Transferring Information

The first and most historically obvious characteristic of the Web environment is that it is an excellent way to manage and transfer information. In the early history of Web use in education, many teachers thought that because the Web made information management and transfer easy and fun, all they had to do was shovel their syllabi and lecture notes into a Web space and students would learn. This made the Web a virtual repository of passive teaching strategies. According to Dr. Curtis Bonk, online teaching guru at Indiana University-Bloomington, "While one can upload one's syllabus and lecture notes to the Web, these are often static, informational documents that seldom foster reflection or change in one's pedagogy." ("Teaching on the Web" 15).

Although students may learn by informational transfer, the primary focus of informational transfer is on the information and *not* on the learner. When instructors focus on supplying information to students, the students tend to become mere receptacles for that information. This encourages rote learning and minimizes reflective critical thinking. In order to take the student beyond mere informational transfer, in the classroom or on the Web, learning activities must be designed to put the learner in the center of the learning experience.

A well-designed online course demands a *learner-centered* approach (learning that places the responsibility for learning directly on the student, rather than the teacher) because students must learn independently due to the physical absence of the teacher, classroom and classmates. Good independent learners naturally engage in the process of learning, as well as in the content, because they are ultimately responsible for their own learning. Students who are not normally motivated to engage in the process of learning can be helped to become active learners if the course materials are developed with an active pedagogy. The Web environment, with its never-ending supply of information and ideas, becomes a learning environment only when students *interact* with it. *As online course developers, it is our job to create opportunities for students to interact with the course content.* In this way, we are no longer the "sage on the stage," simply dispensing information to our students. Instead, we become "the guide on the side," coaching our students to discover, build, share, apply and reflect on the information available to them through our course content and beyond.

Active learning requires that students discover, build, share, apply and reflect on information rather than just receive it. *Active learning*, according to Randal Carlson and Judi Repman, is defined as "learner involvement with both the instructional content and learning processes." Constructivist psychology includes the requirement that the learner interact with real-world situations to shape meaning (Carlson 7). Below are examples of some active-learning assignments appropriate to a public speaking course. (Note the Compendium of Online Activities on pages 29-48 contains specific chapter-by-chapter examples of active learning exercises.)

- Your oral speaking assignments can be structured to accommodate skills or types of speaking needed in the "real world," such as an informational speech to explain a technical problem or subject, or a persuasive speech to influence change on a question of policy.
- Homework assignments, such as "What Should Felicia Do?" on page 33 in the Compendium of Online Activities, offer students the opportunity to think through a real-world problem and apply ethical concepts from the text.
- Using a class forum promotes active learning by making the results of learning public and relevant to others. The "Database Discovery" exercise on page 36 of the Compendium gives students the opportunity to discover and share information

on new and exciting databases with the whole class.
- The "Sleuth the Sites" activity on page 37 of the Compendium requires students to use their investigative and evaluative skills to discover which website is most worthy for academic use.
- Using a speech from the Lucas Student CD-ROM, have students identify different aspects or parts of the speech (such as introduction, body, conclusion, transition, specific purpose, linguistic devices, etc.) or note specific linguistic devices.

These examples are considered active because students are placed in a learner-centered position, and are asked to discover information by reading, viewing, listening and reflecting, sharing, and applying. Students are not objects of informational transfer from teacher to student. Active learning increases student engagement with the material and encourages retention.

A well-designed Web learning environment, with its potentially vast array of tools and informational media, strongly supports active learning. By designing your online course using active-learning strategies, such as relevant speaking assignments, critical reflection on real-life problems, group or partnership projects, and forum discussions, you not only maximize the learning potential of the Web, but you also position yourself to get out of the way and let students engage themselves in the real process of learning.

These reasons give rise to *Course Design Principle No. 1*: **Using active rather than passive learning strategies puts students in the center of the online learning paradigm.**   (All of these principles are listed in Figure 3.)

2)   An Environment with an Absence of Regular Face-to-Face Contact

Another obvious characteristic of an online environment is the absence of regular face-to-face contact. Online students experience a sense of isolation or "psychological distance" from the teacher and from each other unless the course designer provides for frequent social interaction within the course. Online students, who come to class only to give speeches or meet infrequently as part of the online class, need a way to give and receive social support from each other and from the teacher on a consistent basis during the semester.

Traditional classroom learning communities, occurring with increasing frequency on campuses throughout the country, were created to provide a framework for students to connect with others. Such learning communities build meaning and self-identity, and allow students to share and construct knowledge. The need for a learning community, and the social interaction it provides, is just as important in a Web-based learning environment. The problem is that the social element is not as inherent online as it is in a face-to-face classroom setting—it must be engineered deliberately and embedded into the design of the online course.

In Web-based courses without the social element, students may not feel safe expressing themselves because they are physically isolated from each other most, if not all, of the time. It is hard to feel part of a group of people you cannot see, and even harder to feel the trust necessary for meaningful interaction. This may limit interaction, and encourage *lurking* (being online and observing others in chats or discussions, but not participating) and subsequent disengagement from course content.

Students may also feel invisible. This is a disaster for students who are extroverts or whose *learning styles* (a preferred way of perceiving and processing information) require frequent interaction with teacher and classmates. It is so easy for these learners to stop participating or drop the class because they were no more than a name to the instructor and the rest of the class. On the other hand, a sense of invisibility may not bother shy, reticent introverts. Such people may delight in the invisibility of the online classroom and may blossom away from the peer pressures that exist in a traditional classroom.

Whatever the case, as online course designers, we must provide the opportunity for structured social interaction in the absence of physical presence because it is crucial to effective, quality learning. If the social needs of students aren't satisfied, the consequences are lack of engagement with the material and unusually high attrition, which is all too common in Web-based courses. Instructors can help students feel more comfortable and stimulate intellectual discussion by e-mailing students frequently and making sure feedback on assignments is given in a timely fashion. Students can help each other engage in the course material if they are given a place to discuss social and intellectual issues, and if they are able to participate in assignments as groups or partners.

For these reasons, two principles emerge:

Online Course Design Principle No. 2: **Using frequent, timely and personable interaction via e-mail and reflective comments on homework builds crucial student-teacher relationships that contribute to intellectual and social engagement in the course.**

Online Course Design Principle No. 3: **Embedding social interaction within assignments by using partnerships, group work, discussion forums, debates, chats, electronic cafes, etc., stimulates student-student interaction and engagement in content.**

3)   A Medium Based on the Written Word

Another characteristic of the Web is that it is based on the written word, and as such, is an excellent medium by which to convey written communication of ideas. With the exception of *chats* (real time synchronous informational transfer on the Web) most of this written communication is asynchronous. The delay in sending and receiving messages, homework essays, threaded group conferencing, etc., can be advantageous because students are able to take the time to reflect and craft more well-thought-out responses. Students can be challenged to organize, analyze, synthesize and share through the written word. As the instructor, you may find student essays and discussion comments crucial to monitoring the initial intellectual levels and subsequent intellectual progress of your students prior to the times you hear their speeches. Student responses to critical-thinking questions, like those in *The Art of Public Speaking*'s "Exercises for Critical Thinking" and "Applying the Power of Public Speaking," are excellent indicators of the extent of student learning. You will discover right away who your critical thinkers are and who may need help. Likewise, you must take the time to craft a well-worded, constructive response to student work that encourages further thought development.

Therefore, *Online Course Design Principle No. 4* is crucial: **Including written homework assignments to encourage critical reflection and taking the time to respond to student work in a way that stimulates further thought are necessary parts of the process.**

4)   A Resource of Tools, Information and Media

A final characteristic is that the Web contains a mind-boggling array of tools, information and media. Having an information super-highway at one's fingertips is an instructor's dream. Course designers have the ability to use a variety of media and informational options to create a course that appeals to students with different learning styles. The use of streaming video and audio, *interactive websites* (websites that provide opportunities for students to act and react with the content and process of the site), archived speeches, and *webcasts* (video broadcasts via the Internet), as well as material contained on the Lucas Student CD-ROMs, in the McGraw-Hill Online Learning Center and PowerWeb (www.mhhe.com/lucas8), provides active-learning opportunities that go far beyond simply reading a textbook. The disadvantage is, in the face of this wealth of technology, it is easy to want to incorporate as many bells and whistles as possible in course design. However, best practice indicates that pedagogy should be the driving force behind the use and choice of technology and not vice versa.

These elements give rise to ***Online Course Design Principle No. 5***: **Using a variety of media and technology helps course assignments appeal to a diversity of learning styles, but make sure that the choice of technology is driven by sound pedagogy.**

Figure 3
Web Course Design Principles

Course Design Principle No. 1:
Using active, rather than passive, learning strategies puts students in the center of the online learning paradigm.

Course Design Principle No. 2:
Using frequent, timely and personable interaction via e-mail and reflective comments on homework builds crucial student-teacher relationships that contribute to intellectual and social engagement in the course.

Course Design Principle No. 3:
Embedding social interaction within assignments by using partnerships, group work, discussion forums, debates, chats, electronic cafes, etc., stimulates student-student interaction and engagement in content.

Course Design Principle No. 4:
Including written homework assignments encourages critical reflection and taking the time to respond to student work in a way that stimulates further thought are necessary parts of the process.

Course Design Principle No. 5:
Using a variety of media and technology helps course assignments appeal to a diversity of learning styles, but make sure that the choice of technology is driven by pedagogy.

Next we'll turn to a discussion of the actual process of course development by suggesting a general procedure to follow. Facilities, opportunities and courses differ from institution to institution, so you may have to modify this design plan to fit your teaching situation.

The Process of Course Development

In conversations with colleagues throughout the country, I discovered that there are three basic types of Web courses in public speaking:

- *Totally online*: computer-mediated delivery of content, taped speeches and little or no face-to-face contact.
- *Mixed mode*: computer-mediated delivery of content and instruction, and face-to-face delivery of most, if not all, of the speeches.
- *Adjunct*: Web is used as an informational, supportive delivery system only, and the method of instruction takes place off-line either in class, by voice mail, by instructional tapes, etc.

Since institutional and teaching situations are different, the following section is a suggested general development process, courtesy of IUPUI instructional designers. The remarks assume that your Web platform is integral to the type of learning environment described in the first two types of courses above.

The flow chart in Figure 4 suggests an order of task completion.

Figure 4
Course Development Flow Chart

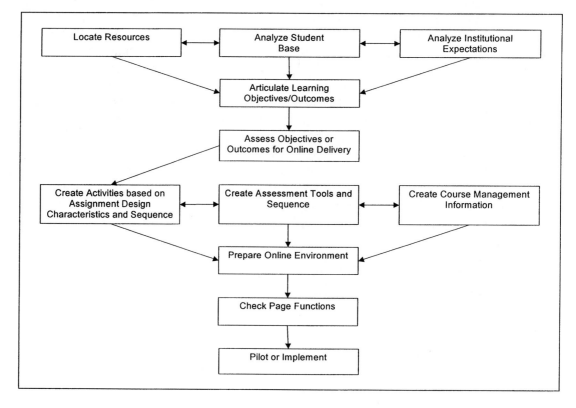

Locate Resources

Before you do anything else, seek out help with your online course development. Consider such resources as peers, your department, your institution or area institutions, websites, books and journals. A checklist of the various resources is provided in Figure 5.

Your Peers: There may be faculty members at your school and at other institutions who have developed communication courses online. Talk to those people. Look at their websites. They will provide valuable insight into the nature of your undertaking. Colleagues from other disciplines can be of great help as well. While talking with instructors around the country who have put their basic speech courses online, I found that almost all of them voiced the desire to talk to other instructors about their online course development and about their teaching and learning experiences. See the acknowledgments for a limited list of these people. All of them have had the experience of using *The Art of Public Speaking* in their online public speaking courses.

Your Department: Your department may provide you with funds or release time, enabling you to easily pursue your goal. Recognize that this project may take as much as one year to implement. Ask your Chair or your Dean about your options for grants or fellowships.

Your Institution and Other Institutions: Your institution or nearby area institutions may offer professional or graduate seminars in online course development. You may have access to a team of instructional and technical designers through a center for faculty development or instructional technology unit.

Online Resources: Other resources can be discovered online. Visit Florida Gulf Coast University's online course design document for faculty at http://www.fgcu.edu. Check out University of Central Florida at http://pegasus.cc.ucf.edu/~rite, University of Illinois at http://www.uillinois.edu and Penn State at http://www.psu.edu. All have documents related to online teaching and learning. The Multimedia Educational Resource for Learning Online and Training website (http://www.merlot.org) is a virtual smorgasbord of articles on teaching and learning at a distance. Use keywords such as distance education, course development, faculty development, and distributed education.

Print Resources: There are also some fine books and journals on this subject. Sarah Horton's *Web Teaching Guide* and Horton and Patrick Lynch's *Web Style Guide* address online course design from an instructional and technical point of view. McGraw-Hill offers several books, such as *You Can Teach Online!* by Moore et al., which was written by educators who have put courses in a Web-based format. These books go into much greater detail, answering design and technical questions that are not addressed here. For a more complete list of books and journal articles, see the Suggested Readings section at the end of this book.

Figure 5
Resources to Help You With Your Online Course
Development

Peers
 	
    Faculty – Your Department/Institution
    Faculty – Other institutions
    Faculty – Other disciplines

Department
 	
    Funds for development –Grants and
    fellowships
    Release time

Institutions – Home or Other
 	
    Graduate seminars
    Training sessions
    Instructional design consultants
    Technical design consultants
    Faculty development centers

Online Resources
 	
    Universities
    Businesses and government
    Individual courses
    Consortia

Print Resources
 	
    Books
    Journal Articles
    Newspapers, Magazines, Book Reviews

Analyze Your Student Base

Just as you would do with any speech, you should have a feeling for the characteristics of the student "audience" that may be taking your course. Consider:

- Who will take the course? Consider factors like age, gender ratio, race, marital status, first-generation college students, full/part-time students, business people, etc.
- From what geographical area you will be drawing students? Will this affect the characteristics of your traditional student base?
- What is the general educational level of your potential students?
- What is the general level of technical expertise of your potential students?
- What percentage has taken online courses previously?
- What is their purpose for taking your course?

Answers to these questions will help you create your assignments with the greatest benefit to the students. Knowing the general technical expertise and equipment availability of your student base will dictate what levels of technology you will be able to use in your course. The instructional and technological sophistication of your course may change slightly as your area develops a student base that is experienced in taking online courses. These phenomena will affect your choices as you put your course together.

Analyze Institutional Expectations For Your Course

In an institutional sense, it is important that you know your institution's expectations for your course and student enrollment. Talk to your Dean or Chair about such questions as:

- Will your course fulfill a general education requirement? Will it be fully transferable to other institutions in its online form? Will it satisfy the requirements of different schools or programs within your institution in its online form?
- Will your course be subject to open enrollment (i.e., anyone can sign up)? If not, how will students be selected into your online section? Are there prerequisites?

General Education Requirement: If your course satisfies the general education requirement for your school, you will probably have your course objectives prescribed for you. You will want to take great pains to see that the online section teaches the same skills as the traditional classes, so that it is fully transferable from an institutional perspective, as well as from the standpoint of various programs, schools or units within your institution.

Initially at IUPUI, the School of Education did not allow their majors to take the online public speaking course because mistakenly, they thought an online course meant there was no face-to-face component, which is a crucial element to their teacher training. Since the course *does* offer the face-to-face element, the misunderstanding was cleared up. How your course is structured, whether totally or partially online, may affect who is able to enroll in it. Make sure the advisors and counselors in your institution understand the structure and specifications of your online class.

Open Enrollment: If you have open enrollment, you may encounter a host of problems, as students inexperienced with online learning sign up for your class bearing unrealistic expectations. It's important that you determine who will be able to sign up for your course. Because online learning is in its infancy and people don't understand it, many regard it with stereotypical notions. In the communication discipline, for example, many students—particularly students with high communication apprehension—sign up for an online public speaking class because they think it will be easier or will get them out of having to speak in front of a live audience. Whatever their fears, dealing with these students from a distance is an immense challenge, and you will have to plan for it.

Open enrollment may cause you to have to deal with students for whom online learning is not their best learning method. A host of difficulties, such as poor writing skills, insufficient technical skills, poor time management, and inadequate mastery of the English language may complicate learning online. Dealing with these problems in a traditional class is hard enough. Online delivery compounds them and may result in poor retention and/or poor work on the part of the student, and a great deal more work for the instructor.

Some institutions offer training sessions for students who sign up for online courses. These seminars teach students how to navigate the courseware that is used for the online class and may deal with other aspects of learning online. Other institutions may not have this luxury, and instructors find themselves having to train students by offering some kind of instruction during face-to-face class time or in an online tutorial. Whether or not you or your institution offer student training will affect the time you spend with each student, answering, explaining, coaxing and prodding.

If you have the freedom to select who is in your online section, a distance-learning survey will be helpful. To get students thinking about how best they learn, IUPUI provides a survey that briefly assesses students' learning style and technical knowledge. The results are sent directly to my e-mail account, and I use them to interview the student. The survey is not a predictor of success. However, the answers help me determine whether the student would be a good candidate for the section. (See the Sample Distance Learning Survey on page 55.)

Knowing the purpose of your course and who will or can take it will directly affect what you put into your course as you develop it.

Articulate Your Learning Objectives

You will be light-years ahead if you have your course objectives or learning outcomes and requirements already mapped out. Your objectives should be clearly stated and measurable. An example of course objectives and learning outcomes can be found in Figure 6.

Objectives Should Be Clearly Stated: At IUPUI, the Principles of Undergraduate Learning (PUL) (http://www.universitycollege.iupui.edu//UL/Principles.htm), upon which all university courses are based, are crucial to course design. The general education course, The Fundamentals of Speech Communication, was redesigned around the PUL. A department faculty task force decided the type and number of speeches and made recommendations on other course requirements, such as outside speaker reports, participation in our Speech Night contest, etc. As the course was converted to a Web-delivered format, the development team ensured that the course objectives and speaking opportunities were as similar as possible to the traditional course so that it would be fully transferable.

Objectives Should Be Measurable: Learning outcomes should be measurable. Naturally they should be stated from the standpoint of student learning. Stating your outcomes in this fashion will give you a solid feel for what assignments you should include in your syllabus and if and how the outcome can realistically be measured.

Figure 6
Sample Statements of Chapter Objectives
and Learning Outcomes

Chapter 13 Objectives – *The Art of Public Speaking*	Individual Course Learning Outcome – Your Course
• Explain the major advantages of using visual aids in a speech.	• Choose and incorporate appropriate technology in speech making.
• Identify the kinds of visual aids available for use in speeches.	• Prepare an effective transparency or slide using text.
• Apply the guidelines given in the chapter for preparing and presenting visual aids.	• Prepare an effective transparency or slide using charts, graphs or pictures.

Assess Objectives For Online Delivery

The most important question to ask in the communication discipline is, "What objectives in your course *must* be handled face-to-face?" The question has to be asked even if you are teaching for a university that requires you to teach your course totally online. The answer, plus your teaching situation, will dictate how you create the environment for face-to-face work.

For example, if you are not allowed to meet with students personally, you will need to consider how to structure the speaking assignments so that students have the opportunity to speak in front of a live audience. How you will personally evaluate the progress of these students is also a big consideration. Or, if you are allowed limited class meeting times, you will need to think of which speeches you will hear and which might be done by other means. Think about the other portions of your course that are not oral. Consider whether these outcomes can be satisfied or enhanced by online delivery. This is the part of your course development that will challenge your creativity. The good news is that there are interesting ways to satisfy the oral and non-oral outcomes. They may not be the same as in your traditional classes. They may produce unintended consequences. They may surprise you with their results.

The next section will discuss the characteristics of successful online course assignments. Before creating your course assignments, revisit your objectives and learning outcomes. At this point, you should know what courseware you will be using because the capabilities of your courseware will determine what tools you have available to design your course activities. You may have access to a sophisticated array of technological tools outside of your courseware as well. Whatever you have, please make sure that your pedagogy drives your choice of technology and not vice versa.

Create Activities With Assignment Design Characteristics In Mind

The American Distance Education Consortium (ADEC) has created a list of Guiding Principles for Distance Teaching and Learning (http://www.adec.edu/admin/papers/distance-teaching_principles.html). These principles, along with the course design principles explained in the section, Changing the Web Environment into a Learning Environment, have crucial implications for course and assignment design. While the Course Design Principles are meant to help you use Web characteristics to design a Web learning environment, the following individual *assignment* characteristics provide you with more information on how to create your individual class activities.

The following course assignment characteristics are based on the ADEC Guiding Principles:

1) Assignments should be learner centered, promoting active engagement with the content and the process.

As you think about exercises and activities that will satisfy your learning outcomes, ask yourself by what method you have traditionally satisfied them. For instance, if you normally lecture on the topic of audience analysis and your students do little more than receive this information (hopefully putting it to good use later), you have been teaching in a manner that promotes *passive learning*. Passive learning is learning by informational transfer from teacher to student—the student is considered a "receiver" of information. Instead, ask how you can create an opportunity for students to "discover" or "build" this same information for themselves and process it in a way that leads to preparation of more effective speeches. If you already use active learning (defined on page 10 and in the glossary), or *collaborative learning* (learning done in groups or partnerships) in your classroom, you may have an activity that could be converted to an online assignment quite easily.

2) All activities and assignments should be tied directly to learning outcomes/objectives.

Course objectives, learning outcomes and their corresponding assignments and means for assessment should be communicated clearly to the students before and during the class. This offers precise course goals to the students and the means for reaching them. It allows students to understand how they will be assessed and by what criteria.

In the Compendium of Online Activities (page 29) you will find that each assignment is tied to a chapter objective in the Lucas textbook.

3) Assignments should appeal to diverse learning styles.

Web teaching gives us the opportunity to use a fantastic variety of media that appeal to a variety of learning styles. *The Art of Public Speaking,* the CD-ROMs that accompany the text, the McGraw-Hill Online Learning Center with the new Public Speaking PowerWeb (http://www.mhhe.com/lucas8), and other ancillaries allow access to course materials that appeal to the visual, auditory and kinesthetic learning modalities. The Internet may provide links to other sites with interactive activities that will engage diverse learning styles.

Public speaking classes normally create the opportunity for active assignments that foster critical thinking, critical listening and evaluation, ethical listening, and implementation of theory through the actual giving of speeches and utilization of tools that support speaking, such as audio/video equipment, PowerPoint, etc. As you convert your traditional course to online delivery or create your new course, you should seek to maintain as many of these active-learning strategies as possible.

4) Assignments should foster critical thinking and construction of new knowledge through both knowledge-based and problem-based learning activities.

Because the computer environment lends itself well to reflective writing, assigning essays or discussion forums based on questions similar to those in Lucas' "Applying the Power of Public Speaking" and the "Exercises for Critical Thinking," gives your students multiple opportunities to engage in critical thinking. You may want to create original questions on the readings in the text, on outside readings, or on the viewing of a student or famous speech. Another strategy for promoting critical thinking may include "What Did I Learn?"—a short paragraph stating what the student learned after a given part of the course or certain speech assignment. Additional ideas include mock trials or debates, case-based reasoning discussions, comparison and contrast essays, etc. (See Bonk, "Learner-Centered" 171.)

Naturally, the speeches you assign give students ample opportunity to practice these higher-order thinking skills through audience analysis, synthesis and organization of researched material, and the actual oral application of the same. Audience analysis papers, preparation outlines, self-evaluations, peer evaluations, and evaluations of outside speakers are all opportunities to foster reflective critical thought.

5) Assignments should include social interaction, collaboration and cooperation.

If learning is indeed a social activity and is measured in social/real-world contexts, it is crucial that we create a learning environment that allows for learning with and from other people.

The forced isolation of online students from each other and from the instructor works against the social nature of learning, causing high attrition in online courses. The speech anxiety inherent in a public speaking course compounds the problem. Students need to feel comfortable communicating with others in the class. They should have the opportunity to find friends for support during the time they are in class together. Structured interaction gives your students a sense of class community that is not inherent in the virtual classroom.

For example, Del Wakely suggests creating open discussion areas or cafes to encourage students to make friends online (8). I have created La Trattoria, an online forum area that serves as an initial class meeting venue where students describe themselves, ask questions, voice concerns and respond to each other. Creating forum discussions of questions or events can easily encourage this type of interaction.

Activities that require your students to work together in groups or partnerships, and learn from each other online, reinforce the learner-centered socialization and interaction necessary for active learning on the Web. Ideally your courseware will allow formation of small groups for cooperative projects to be discussed. Assignments, such as group reviews of outside readings or group critiques of famous or student speeches, are examples of engaging ways for individuals to learn from and with each other.

Other activities involve partners, asynchronous or synchronous discussions, structured debates, etc. (Bonk, "Learner-Centered" 173)

6) Assignments should be presented in modules, chunks or units.

According to Sarah Horton (45), a "peculiarity of the Web is that readers generally do not read pages in a sequence." She states that although authors of novels can be fairly certain that a reader who has read page 32 probably has read page 31, readers of Web pages cannot be trusted to read in such a sequential fashion. Even if the Web author has provided page links, the reader cannot be forced to follow them. As a result, the effective Web author must provide information in short, easily absorbed "chunks," or stand alone units, which allow the reader to find the information quickly, process it, and/or print out the salient information. Although this phenomenon applies to general Web design, it also gives us direction for creating and formatting our assignments, activities and exercises in chunks that are easily absorbed.

For excellent examples of this design concept, see Lynch's *Web Style Guide* and *You Can Teach Online*, Moore et al.

7) Activities should be effectively supported by your courseware.

It is important for you to understand the capabilities of your courseware as you create your assignments. For example, a great collaborative group exercise will fall short if your courseware is difficult or too complicated to use or doesn't allow students to work privately in small online group areas.

8) Assignments should contain internal assessment features.

Because students easily disappear at the end of an online course, if you wait until the end of the term to use a post-course assessment tool, you may be disappointed with the response unless you tie the assessment to a consequence. It is actually better to build in assessments of the objectives during the course because it will tip you off to poor student work or students who are struggling. Pedagogically speaking, continuous assessment fosters increased engagement with the content as students seek to demonstrate what they've learned on an on-going basis.

Public speaking lends itself quite well to periodic assessment because of the intermittent speaking assignments. You will be assessing students' progress by listening to their speeches at certain points in the semester and by reading papers that reflect what they have learned, such as self-evaluation essays after each speech or essays that address the critical thinking questions at the ends of chapters. If you are teaching a class that comes together to hear speeches in person, requiring oral and written peer evaluations will give you a solid feel for the progress your students are making in the area of critical listening and in their understanding of communication theory. You may also create a suggestion box online or just ask the students up front about an assignment. You can use student complaints or confusion as a sign that a certain assignment may need tweaking. If your courseware has a test tool, you can use this to assess students' reading comprehension. Threaded discussions, group projects, reviews and chats will allow you to measure student thinking and understanding during the course. If possible, ask other faculty to review your choice of exercises and activities. The feedback you receive may lead you to modify your assignments or generate new ideas. (The following section provides additional information about assessment.)

Assess Course Learning Outcomes

If active learning on the Web suggests engagement with the process of learning, as well as with the content (Carlson 7), then it follows that course design must include active assessment strategies that involve students demonstrating what they have learned.

According to instructional management systems consultant Sharon Shuey (17):

> "Assessment should be an ongoing process, integrated throughout the course, and not seen as providing a simple grade at the conclusion of the course. It's planning and approach is critical to the design and implementation. It serves as the key to effective student performance by setting standards and criteria in advance and communicating these to students. As learners, students need to know clearly and specifically what is expected of them in order to achieve a successful outcome."

Shuey goes on suggest that by using a variety of outcome-driven strategies (both graded and ungraded), teachers are better able to identify excellent or inconsistent work.

Most public speaking courses (not just those that are online) typically offer instructors a multitude of practical ways to assess learning outcomes. The opportunities we give our students to demonstrate their oral delivery, audience adaptation, organization, research, group process, and evaluative skills in class or on tape are inherent in any public speaking or hybrid communication course. For an online course, instructors also can ask for student evaluation of assignments after speeches, projects or other major portions of the course by using a suggestion box, an outside faculty facilitator, or a series of questions that can be answered anonymously using a pseudonym.

However, prior to the actual presentation of speeches, it will be necessary to assess student progress in knowledge and understanding of rhetorical concepts and communication theory. Appropriate ways to assess this kind of learning during the course include critical thinking papers, threaded discussions, chats, partner or group projects, and structured debates.

Using selected-answer or constructed-response testing tools (tests and quizzes), which are easily convertible from a traditional course, may tell you only that the student has done the reading. Although this type of testing has its place in education, it lends itself more to rote learning and does not fit in well with effective online learning, which should motivate students to actively prove their mastery of the material.

Shuey (15) suggests these general criteria for effective online assessment:

- Assessment strategies should be continuous, integral, paced and systematic and require deadlines for completion.
- Timely feedback from the instructor is key to assessment effectiveness.
- Assessment strategies should be tied directly to learning outcomes and clearly communicated.
- Whenever possible, students should be given a variety of options for assessment.

Even though you may be required to assess your course using department, school or institutional instruments at the end of your course, by creating your strategies based on outcomes, applying them strategically, and giving students a choice of active assessment options, you will be creating a more effective and engaging online learning environment.

Sequence Your Course Activities And Assessment Tools

Once you have created assignments to satisfy your course objectives, you must give thought to making a schedule of assignments.

Assuming you know in what order and at what point in the semester you want your speeches, homework, tests, etc., to be scheduled, best practice will dictate that you divide your schedule into units, groups, categories or logical chunks (Horton 45). This makes it easier for the student to access and process the information.

There are as many ways to organize your schedule as there are instructors. Your courseware may dictate the design of your schedule. (See examples in Lynch and Horton, Horton, and Moore et al., and Sample Course Schedule on page 59.)

However you organize the assignments, make sure that the narrative is as succinct as possible without compromising understanding. Also, don't assign too many activities to satisfy each objective. Remember that everything you assign, you will have to evaluate, grade, or deal with in some manner. Whatever is more work for your students is also more work for you.

Create Course Management Information

Course management is the information that organizes the web-based course. It usually includes policies and procedures related to the delivery of assignments and other "housekeeping" tasks. Included in management content would be items such as:

Introduction to the Course:
- Course description
- Welcome letter
- Course goals
- Contact information
- Materials and supplies
- Getting started page
- Tips for learning online

Course Policies:
- Participation
- Speech and written grading criteria, and the grading scale
- Communication: *netiquette* (rules for communicating via e-mail), e-mail turnaround time, online discussions and *flaming* (negative, inflammatory e-mail designed to influence opinion)
- Homework submission procedures and back-up plans
- Plagiarism, cheating and online testing integrity
- Policies for make-up speeches, tests and assignments

Assignment Information:
- Speaking dates
- Taping requirements
- Preparation outline and other writing criteria
- Topic approval
- Assignment descriptions
- Bibliographical requirements

Student Services:
- Tutoring services and speaker's lab
- Technical training
- Online learning training
- Learning platform tutorial
- Online learning survey
- Campus resources
- Technical resources

Whatever you decide to include, this text is a significant chunk of information and should be kept separate from the schedule of activities. It should be very easy to access, read and print. (See Sample Course Management Information on page 51.)

Prepare Your Online Environment

Whether you will be working with the assistance of instructional and/or technical designers or creating your own website, you will have given thought to the look, feel and navigability of your online environment throughout the development of the course. This is the point at which you make a list of course content and decide how to present the content in a visual framework. If you are working with a specific courseware platform, like Web CT, Blackboard or PageOut, some of this will have been determined for you. You can get ideas from the websites of colleagues or from journal articles in the Suggested Readings section. Don't forget to revisit Horton's *Web Teaching Guide* and Lynch and Horton's *Web Style Guide*, as well as *You Can Teach Online!* by Moore et.al. These authors explain design concepts that are easy to read and understand for even for the most technically challenged individual.

If you are technically savvy, you may be able to dive right into the technical process of putting your course up online. If you aren't, you may have the option of taking a course, using one-on-one consultation with your designers, or hiring a student or staff person to do it for you. Although the technical work may go faster initially with some help, you may run into problems down the line because you have not mastered the authoring tools. This was my experience, and, as a result, I had to spend time during my summer months to learn the course authoring tools. My suggestion is that you learn as much as you can up-front, so that before the semester begins you can perform course maintenance without having to rely on someone else.

Check Course Functions

Once you have everything in place and before the class begins, check all the spelling, formatting, pages, links and downloads and make sure everything is operational. Keep detailed notes on where things need to be fixed or fix them immediately.

Ideally, you should subject your course pages to the detailed scrutiny of faculty, technical staff and student review. They should check for non-operational links, typos, consistency and correctness of dates, language clarity and other site mistakes.

Pilot Or Implement Your Course

If you have the luxury of piloting the course with a small student population, do it. The advantage of piloting is that it gives you a chance to get all the bugs worked out, both technically and pedagogically. If you don't have this luxury, go full steam ahead into the semester. Be sure to let your students know that this is the first time for this course and for you teaching it. Ask them to help you get the bugs worked out. If you communicate this up front, the students will be very helpful. Once the course is in session, consider these instructional tips:

- **Budget the time you spend online with your course**. The first time you teach, you may find yourself spending huge amounts of time in front of the computer. Nervous novices may check e-mail constantly and give almost instant feedback to students. This may set unrealistic expectations for message turnaround time, play havoc with other office or class duties, and/or affect personal relationships at home. Announce to your class what your message turnaround time might be. For example, strive for a 24-hour maximum turnaround time for regular e-mail messages and check e-mail about 3 times a day. If you don't work on Sundays, say so, or check e-mail less often on that day. It is a good idea to tell students when they can expect feedback in the way of grades.

- **Give timely feedback**. If you expect your students to keep up with the work you assign and develop the competencies dictated by your objectives, they will definitely expect you to keep up with the grading and evaluation. It is imperative that students have a solid sense of their progress in the course. Also, the relative isolation of you from your students can be minimized by timely feedback. If your public speaking course is grounded in good evaluation of progress, make sure you deliver that evaluation in a manner that gives students time to do remedial work or proceed to the next assignment with confidence. Research suggests that students judge the worth of an online course by how much interaction they have with the instructor. This is a human touch that will increase the quality, popularity and hopefully the retention in your course.

- **Plan for technical failures.** If students cannot get papers, tests or other assignments submitted because of technical glitches, be calm, courteous and fair. In your course management policies, suggest alternate methods for homework submission, such as faxing. You may want to tell students to call your voice mail should they encounter any difficulty with the courseware or their e-mail. Check and see if your courseware records login, logout, test retrieval and submission times for your students. This data will help you document student claims of technical failure. You may create other backup plans to cover other elements of the course that are subject to technology failure. Just don't begin your course without policies in place to cover these potential problems.

- **Plan for lack of student participation or attendance.** What will you do if you have a limited number of face-to-face meetings scheduled for speeches and your students don't show up? You may find yourself devoting a considerable amount of time to make-up speeches if you don't have a policy in place to cover such things. Do you have deadlines for assignments? What do you do if students don't meet those deadlines? How do you determine student "attendance" in an online class? From an institutional perspective, this may be a critical question in terms of federal financial aid. You might define attendance by the last time you were in contact with the student or when that student submitted homework. Be sure to document student "presence" very carefully. At IUPUI, there is a policy of administrative withdrawal, which means the instructor can withdraw a student from the class if the student has been "present" less than half of the first four weeks of class. In the online class, this means if one-half of the work is not done within the first four weeks, the student is withdrawn involuntarily.

As you continue to teach your online class, the need to create course policy for situations you haven't anticipated will become apparent in a host of ways.

- **Take the time to write personable e-mail messages.** Be encouraging, friendly, upbeat and positive. These types of messages go a long way online. Don't hesitate to reveal your personality and humorous side because it puts a "face" on your messages and gives a human touch to the course.

- **Deal face-to-face with negative feelings**. E-mail is a very poor way to communicate feelings associated with anger and hurt, and e-mail confrontations do not lend themselves to fast or efficient resolution. It is best to meet a problematic student face-to-face or by phone to discuss whatever issues you might be having. If your only option is dealing with the problem via e-mail, be sure to take the time to create an objectively worded message.

The next section describes exercises from *The Art of Public Speaking*, 8th ed., and other sources, which have been converted or modified for use in an online learning environment.

Compendium of Online Activities

The activities in this section are active learning exercises converted from traditional sources for online use. For each chapter you will find one or more activities and the following information:

- The name of the activity
- The related learning objective or outcome
- The source material from which the activity was adapted
- A description of the activity
- Course design principle(s) met by the activity (discussed in Changing the Web Environment into a Learning Environment and listed again in Figure 7)
- Assignment characteristic(s) met by the activity (discussed in The Process of Course Development and listed in Figure 8)
- Tips for using, teaching and grading the activity

The majority of these activities are adapted from activities and exercises in Lucas' *The Art of Public Speaking*, 8th ed.; the Lucas Student CD-ROM, Version 3.0 (particularly Disk Two, which contains the full student speeches); *Selections from The Speech Communication Teacher* (various editions); and the *Instructor's Manual to accompany The Art of Public Speaking*, 8th ed. Other activities are based on original assignments from the online basic course at IUPUI, with a little help from Susan Schlag, Curtis Bonk, Del Wakely and other authors referred to in the Suggested Readings section.

Although the activities in this collection are more representational than exhaustive, you may find that they stimulate you to create activities of your own. As you do so, create ways to foster student-student interaction wherever possible, in order to decrease the psychological distance that is inherent in an online course.

When including activities in your course design, keep in mind the following:

- Don't assign too much. Normally, one assignment per outcome is enough, and sometimes more than one outcome can be satisfied in a single exercise. For some objectives, just reading the textbook may be enough. Remember that what you assign, you have to evaluate. Students expect feedback on everything they submit.
- Balance collaborative activities with individual ones. Any number of the "Exercises for Critical Thinking" and "Applying the Power of Public Speaking" scenarios can be assigned for completion by individuals or modified for collaborative work.
- Remember that unless you have structured the assignment carefully, noting point values for responses based on specific criteria, it may be very difficult to assess such exercises as threaded discussions or synchronous chats.

Whenever possible, choose or create an assignment that requires students to interact with the media, the platform, or the course content in such a way that they must discover, analyze, synthesize, reflect, apply or share information.

Other Lucas Resources

The additional resources listed below are just a few of those that accompany *The Art of Public Speaking*, 8th ed., and may be of special use to you in creating active learning assignments for your Web-based course.

- **The Student CD-ROM, Version 3.0,** that accompanies *The Art of Public Speaking*, 8th ed., was used for several of the activities in this book. It contains features that are conducive to independent, active learning, such as interactive study questions; the Speech Outliner, which guides students through the basic process of organizing and outlining; the new outlining exercises, which present scrambled outlines for students to rearrange in the correct order; and 58 video clips and 11 full student speeches.

- **The Internet Connection**, which appears within each chapter, suggests excellent websites that compliment subjects covered in the text.

- **Online Learning Center with PowerWeb**: Accessible at www.mhhe.com/lucas8, the Online Learning Center provides a wealth of resources that supplement *The Art of Public Speaking*. Among those resources is the Top 100 American Speeches of the 20th Century, which is based on a nationwide survey of 137 communication scholars conducted at the end of 1999 by Stephen Lucas and Martin Medhurst. The speeches were rated on two criteria: rhetorical artistry and historical impact. The list provides at least one link to an online transcript of every speech. Many of the linked websites also furnish historical background about the speech and/or additional links with information about the speaker, speech or occasion. Whenever possible, a link has been provided to a site that contains a full or partial audio presentation of the original speech. The aim in developing the Top 100 website was to provide a readily accessible way for students to learn more about the rich history of public speaking. One way to incorporate the site into class is to have each student give an informative presentation about one of the Top 100 speeches.

In addition, the Online Learning Center is integrated with McGraw-Hill's Public Speaking PowerWeb, which keeps students up-to-date and helps them find topics for their presentations by reprinting recent speeches of public interest, as well as news and journal articles related to current issues and public speaking in general. The PowerWeb also provides weekly updates, links to New York Times articles, and a powerful search engine.

- **PageOut:** PageOut allows instructors to create personal course websites by using a template provided by McGraw-Hill. Even the novice computer user can create a course website—no programming knowledge is necessary. Special features of PageOut include an interactive course syllabus, an online gradebook, online testing, and functionality for posting personal files and discussions. All online content for *The Art of Public Speaking* is supported by Web CT, Blackboard and eCollege.com. For more details, check with a McGraw-Hill representative or visit www. pageout.net.

Figure 7
Web Course Design Principles (Revisited)

Course Design Principle No. 1:
Using active, rather than passive, learning strategies puts students in the center of the online learning paradigm.

Course Design Principle No. 2:
Using frequent, timely and personable interaction via e-mail and reflective comments on homework builds crucial student-teacher relationships that contribute to intellectual and social engagement in the course.

Course Design Principle No. 3:
Embedding social interaction within assignments by using partnerships, group work, discussion forums, debates, chats, electronic cafes, etc., stimulates student-student interaction and engagement in content.

Course Design Principle No. 4:
Including written homework assignments encourages critical reflection and taking the time to respond to student work in a way that stimulates further thought are necessary parts of the process.

Course Design Principle No. 5:
Using a variety of media and technology helps course assignments appeal to a diversity of learning styles, but make sure that the choice of technology is driven by pedagogy.

Figure 8
Course Assignment Characteristics

Course Assignment Principle No. 1:
Assignments should be learner centered, promoting active engagement with the content and the process.

Course Assignment Principle No. 2:
All activities and assignments should be tied directly to learning outcomes/objectives.

Course Assignment Principle No. 3:
Assignments should appeal to diverse learning styles.

Course Assignment Principle No. 4:
Assignments should foster critical thinking and construction of new knowledge through both knowledge-based and problem-based learning activities.

Course Assignment Principle No. 5:
Assignments should include social interaction, collaboration and cooperation.

Course Assignment Principle No. 6
Assignments should be presented in modules, chunks or units.

Course Assignment Principle No. 7
Activities should be effectively supported by your courseware.

Course Assignment Principle No. 8
Assignments should contain internal assessment features.

Compendium Contents

First Day or Pre-Class Activity
"Cyber Café"

Objective: Students should begin to identify and bond with virtual classmates.

Source material: Create a forum discussion area for informal social conversation. (Refer to Del Wakely's article in Resources for more ideas.)

Description: Ask students to describe themselves in no more than three sentences and then either comment about a concern they have in the course or ask a question.

Course Design Principle(s): Principles #2 and #3—socialization is embedded in the assignment.

Assignment Design Characteristic(s): #5—if students are encouraged to interact with each other and with you on an informal basis, they may feel more comfortable communicating with each other during the course. Psychological distance may be lessened. Hopefully this interaction will lead to depth and more frequency of communication with regard to course content.

Teaching Tips: This activity is delightful because students' responses are short and easy-to-read and does not need to be graded. It will give you insight into the class personalities, and it can be very entertaining to read how students describe themselves. It is wise to insert an answer right along with the students or artfully comment on their answers if there is time.

Chapter One – Speaking In Public
"Good Speaker/Bad Speaker"

Objective: Students should identify and reflect upon effective and ineffective public speaking behaviors of themselves and others.

Source material: Based on "Exercises for Critical Thinking" #2 and #3 in *The Art of Public Speaking*, 8th ed., p. 29.

Description: In a forum discussion area, ask students to list five characteristics of effective and ineffective speakers *without mirroring their answers* (for example, students may tend to say "an effective speaker has good eye contact," and "an ineffective speaker does not have good eye contact"). At the end of their lists, ask them to briefly identify their own strengths and weaknesses and state two-three things they want to work on during your class. You may ask them to comment on at least one other answer.

Course Design Principle(s): #3–embedded student socialization and interaction; and #4–critical reflection.

Assignment Design Characteristics: #2-#5

Teaching Tips: If you do not have a face-to-face orientation, this makes an excellent first formal assignment. Don't make it worth too many points because you want the students to practice using the forum and have fun giving answers that are non-threatening to others and self-revelatory. It is a good way to get students to think about public speaking and talk to each other about it. Their anxiety levels are high at this point, and you may find this a good way for highly anxious students to connect with each other. This is a short assignment to read and grade because it consists of two short lists and several sentences at the end.

This activity can be completed before or after students read Chapter One. If students complete it before they read the chapter, they are not as likely to parrot the book and may surprise you with the depth of their answers. This activity also gives students a sense of who is in their class and what their thoughts and inadequacies might be. They will find great comfort and possible camaraderie in this, particularly if your class is totally online and you ask them to encourage or comment on at least one other student answer.

Chapter Two – Ethics and Public Speaking

"What Should Felicia Do?"

Objective: Students should be able to identify and discuss five guidelines for ethical speechmaking presented in the chapter.

Source material: Based on "Exercises for Critical Thinking" #1 in *The Art of Public Speaking*, 8th ed., p. 51.

Description: Ask students to revisit the story of Felicia Robinson in the text. Have students put themselves in the role of Felicia's campaign adviser and explain what would be the most ethical course of action for Felicia to take, backing up their advice by specifically referring to the five ethical guidelines. Students should post their primary answer in the forum, and if instructed, comment on the answers of one or two others in the class.

Course Design Principle(s): This activity is done as a threaded forum discussion, and as such, satisfies Principle #3 by embedding student-student interaction; and #4, critical reflection on a real-world problem. If you choose to comment on each answer, this activity also satisfies #2 by fostering student-teacher interaction.

Assignment Design Characteristics: #1-#5

Teaching Tips: Students enjoy this exercise because they can apply what they are reading to a real-world problem. The answers are enjoyable to read because they reveal a lot about the intellectual levels and ethics of the students in the class. It is easy to grade their primary answers; however, if students are asked to comment on one or two others, evaluation for grading purposes may be more difficult, if not impossible. You can join the discussion at any point, weaving ideas together, challenging student answers, or sending back private responses. Instructors with large classes may wish to put a word limit on primary answers to ease grading time needed. It is also a good idea to help students comment more insightfully on the remarks of others by asking them to support their points of agreement or disagreement with specific evidence. Hopefully this will decrease useless comments, such as "great answer," "I agree," or "you are way off-base."

Chapter Three – Listening
"Keyword Comprehension"

Objective: Students should be able to listen comprehensively and take notes by the keyword method.

Source material: Based on "Exercises for Critical Thinking" #3 in *The Art of Public Speaking*, 8th ed., p. 71.

Description: Choose a student speech from the Lucas Student CD-ROM, Disk Two, which accompanies the text. Make sure the speech has high interest for the class, and is straightforward and well organized, like the speech on cryonics. Ask students to view the speech and take notes, using the keyword method suggested in the textbook. Have students mark the main ideas in their notes and post their notes as an attachment.

Course Design Principle(s): Because this activity uses the Lucas Student CD-ROM, Version 3.0, it satisfies Principle #5, which calls for using a variety of media to appeal to different student learning styles.

Assignment Design Characteristics: #1-3

Teaching Tips: Fast and easy to grade, this remarkably simple exercise, when done well, can serve as a good lesson in listening that extends beyond itself in two ways. One, students find that learning the keyword method helps them listen in other classes. Two, students who are effective listeners discover that speeches have a definitive organizational structure, which can be visualized by looking at their notes. Some students will actually submit notes that look like an outline. Main points should be easy for them to identify. Depending on the class level and situation, the instructor can add to this assignment by asking students to identify the purpose of the speech and bracket the parts of their notes that correspond to the introduction and conclusion.

This exercise can make a good transition to the next chapter on specific purpose, central idea and main points. At this point, the class could be asked to give a simple introductory speech on tape or in person using the basic organizational concepts of introduction, body (main points) and conclusion.

Chapter Four – Selecting a Topic and Purpose

"Tweak the Topic; Post the Purpose"

Because the learning outcomes in this chapter are so crucial to speech preparation, any of the "Exercises for Critical Thinking" and "Applying the Power of Public Speaking" activities will help to satisfy the outcomes when students complete and post the activity online as homework.

Many students have difficulty distinguishing the general purpose from the specific purpose and the specific purpose from the central idea, and formulating a specific purpose statement and a central idea according to guidelines in the text. As a result, you may want to assign multiple exercises from these areas. Only one of these exercises is offered here.

Objective: The student should be able to formulate a specific purpose statement and a central idea in accordance with text guidelines.

Source material: Based on "Exercises for Critical Thinking" #1 in *The Art of Public Speaking*, 8th ed., p. 105.

Description: Students should submit a properly formulated specific purpose and central idea for their first oral presentation by posting it online for instructor approval. Instructor also may ask for main points.

Course Design Principle(s): This activity focuses on Principle #2, frequent and timely student-teacher interaction.

Assignment Design Characteristics: #1, #2 and #5

Teaching Tips: Although the process of negotiating a topic and formulating the specific purpose and central idea may require numerous e-mail messages, this allows you to use communication with the student as a pedagogical strategy. Relationships that are built through the give and take of writing, rewriting and tweaking of purpose statements pave the way for more open communication, both oral and written, later on. This may be tedious and time-consuming, but it is well worth the effort.

Chapter Five – Analyzing the Audience

"Genderspeak Speech"

Objective: Students should be able to create and rationalize strategic situational and demographic questions for use in preparing a speech in a real-life situation.

Source material: Based on "Applying the Power of Public Speaking" in *The Art of Public Speaking*, 8th ed., p. 135.

Description: Students assume the role of a well-known university professor who is an expert in gender communication. Respected for research, teaching and writing, the professor is invited to address managers of a large local manufacturing company on the subject of gender communication in the workplace. Students should assume that there are communication issues within the company and that the professor will meet with the Human Resources director to plan the presentation. Students should do the following:

- List three major situational questions to ask the HR director, and explain why you are asking them and how you think the answers will contribute to your speech preparation.
- List three major demographic questions to ask the HR director, and explain, same as above.
- Post as a homework essay online to the instructor.

Course Design Principle(s): This exercise integrates concepts from Chapter Five by stimulating critical reflection on a real-life problem, satisfying design Principle #4.

Assignment Design Characteristics: #1-#4

Teaching Tips: This assignment challenges a student's ability to critically think through the possibilities in this situation. Students who are older and have been in the workplace tend to give very insightful answers. Even though the situation hits at the very heart of audience analysis/adaptation, some students may have trouble doing much more than parroting the book in their answers. With this in mind, it is helpful to ask students to consider the situational analysis first because it increases the likelihood that someone will address the disposition of the audience toward the topic and think to ask the HR director who the audience is and what the communication issues are. Seemingly this would then dictate what demographic questions need to be asked. Make sure you ask the students to explain why they are asking the questions they choose, and relate their explanations specifically to their speech preparation.

You may want to assign this as a formal essay of two or more pages and have students submit it at a time when there is no other major work due.

Chapter Six – Gathering Materials

"Database Discovery"
"Sleuth the Sites"

Database Discovery

Objective: Students should identify and become familiar with the major resources available for researching speeches in the library.

Source material: Based on "Self-Contained Library Tour" by Jean DeHart in *Selections from The Speech Communication Teacher, 1994-96*, p. 61.

Description: Ask each student to go to your university's library (preferable) or a library convenient to him or her. Instruct each student to access a database that they have not previously used (non-Internet). Students should post online, in a public forum area, the following information:

1. Name of database (also put this in the subject line of the message box)
2. Kind of database (general, special, or newspaper)
3. The purpose of the database
4. Where the database is located and how to access it
5. How one would use the database
6. Examples of two sources they found in the database

Students should read all the postings and ask a question of at least one other person.

Course Design Principle(s): Based on Principle #1, this is an active, hands-on exercise that will benefit everyone beyond speech class. Assigning this activity in partnerships would satisfy Course Design Principle #3 for student-student collaboration.

Assignment Design Characteristics: #1-#3 and #5

Teaching Tips: This activity should result in a handy resource for the class with not a lot of extra work on their part, other than to read all the forum postings. You should be able to tell if the activity has had any impact on the students by noting source variety in their speech research bibliographies. Grading is relatively straightforward and doesn't take a lot of time if students answer succinctly but carefully in all six areas.

Partners can be assigned to this exercise, too. One library database, as well as one Internet database or virtual library site, could be assigned to the pair. This is especially helpful to homebound persons, prison inmates, or others who cannot physically access a library.

Sleuth the Sites

Objective: Students should be able to evaluate the credibility of a website.

Source material: Based on "Comparing and Contrasting Websites," prepared by Susan Schlag, IUPUI University Library, for *The R110 Student Coursebook to accompany The Art of Public Speaking*.

Description: Compare and contrast the following sites (or two sites for your choosing):
http://www.martinlutherking.org
http://www.stanford.edu/group/King
By investigating the sites and answering the following questions, students should decide which site is *most appropriate* to use as a resource for a college term paper and explain why:

- **Author:** Who is it? What are the author's credentials? Occupation? Position? Experience? Institutional affiliation? Can you tell?

- **Purpose:** What is the purpose for creating the site?
- **Bias:** Does the information seem slanted or biased? How?
- **Information Source:** How was the data or information collected? Was sound research used? Are sources cited or quoted in their entirety?
- **Conclusions:** What conclusions did the author reach? Are conclusions in line with the data or information presented?
- **Relationship to Other Works:** Compared to other works, is the site in tune with or in opposition to conventional wisdom?
- **Attachments:** Do charts, maps, bibliographies, etc., convey or detract from meaning?
- **Currency:** Is the site dated? When was it last updated?
- **Mechanics:** Does the site contain helpful, working links to other sites? Are there links back to the main page?
- **Organization:** Is identifying information easy to find? Are graphics consistent? Is there a site map?

Course Design Principle(s): This is a hands-on investigative activity that applies the evaluative criteria for websites from the textbook. As such, it satisfies Principle #1 and if assigned to groups or partners, satisfies Principle #2.

Assignment Design Characteristics: #1-#4

Teaching Tips: One of these sites is a seemingly well-designed site that defies conventional wisdom. If the activity is assigned to a group, the group may determine this immediately. Some individuals, however, find this site quite credible. You should study the sites carefully before grading the assignment. Grading, however, is relatively fast, and it is fairly easy to tell who has not spent an adequate amount of time working within each site.

Chapter Seven – Supporting Your Ideas
"Colorful Support"

Objective: The student should be able to identify different types of support materials and what points they support.

Source material: Based on "Exercises for Critical Thinking" #2 in *The Art of Public Speaking*, 8th ed., p. 198.

Description: Choose a straightforward informational speech from the Lucas Student CD-ROM, which also appears in full in the Lucas textbook, such as "Cryonics" or "Multicultural, Multilingual." Ask students first to casually listen to the speech and pay attention to the kinds of examples and other support used by the speaker. Then, after giving the printed text to the students as a Word document, have them do the following:

1. Using the highlighter option on the Toolbar, highlight *examples* in light blue

or aqua, *statistics* in light green, and *testimony* in yellow.

2. Underline the main points that the highlighted materials support.

Students should post this as homework online.

Course Design Principle(s): This is an analytical, investigative exercise that applies information from Chapter 7, and as such, satisfies Principle #1. The variety of media used satisfies Principle #5. Students can either read about types of support or hear examples in a sample speech, but ideally, they should do both.

Assignment Design Characteristics: #1-3

Teaching Tips: This assignment gives students a head start on learning to develop main points with a variety of materials. Once you are familiar with the manuscript, have identified the support material and created a grading plan, the grading is easy and swift if the students have stuck to the color scheme.

Chapter Eight – Organizing the Body of the Speech
Chapter Ten – Outlining the Speech

"Super-structure!"

Objective(s): Students should be able to identify major organizational patterns of main points. Students should be able to organize main points and support material by using proper symbolization, indentation, coordination and subordination in an outline form.

Source material: Based on "Exercises for Critical Thinking" #2 in *The Art of Public Speaking*, 8th ed., p. 221.

Description: This activity combines course objectives from Chapters 8 and 10 and builds upon the activity described previously in Chapter 7. In the Chapter 7 exercise, students were asked to identify the main points and types of supporting materials in a manuscript speech. Using the same speech, ask students to organize their main points and support materials into outline form, using appropriate symbolization, indentation, coordination and subordination. Have students identify and outline main points of the introduction and conclusion and write in the connective statements between the main points. Students may refer to the sample outline in Chapter 10. Post online as homework documents.

Option #1: As described for Chapter 7, but use an entirely different full speech from *The Art of Public Speaking*.

Option #2: As described for Chapters 8 and 10 above, but also have students label specific purpose, central idea, introduction, body, conclusion, transitions and types of support materials.

Option #3: As above, but also have students create a speaking outline from the preparation outline.

Course Design Principle(s): Satisfies Principle #1, because it asks students to actively apply information in the text to create an outline product similar to what they will be asked to generate prior to their speeches.

Assignment Design Characteristics: #1-#3

Teaching Tips: Even though students find this time-consuming (reward them sufficiently), it is a great way for them to learn outlining and organization by taking apart a manuscript and putting it together in outline form. The idea is to "see" the blueprint of a speech they may have already heard. However, creating a speaking outline from someone else's manuscript may produce briefer speaking notes than students would ever think to produce for themselves. You may want to archive good submissions of speaking outlines to refer to when you see that the students' speaking notes have become too cumbersome or inappropriate (while giving their speeches). Once you are familiar with the speech and can readily identify the main points, parts, etc., grading the outlines is fairly swift.

Chapter Nine – Beginning and Ending the Speech
"Start and End"

Objective(s): This activity fulfills all chapter objectives. Students will be able to identify all parts of a speech introduction and conclusion. Students will be able to practice gaining attention in various ways in an introduction and fulfilling the functions of a conclusion.

Source material: Based on the Class Activity in the margin of the Annotated Instructor's Edition of *The Art of Public Speaking*, 8th ed., p. 228.

Description: Divide the class into small (3-5) groups or partners and give all groups access to a document of the same sample student speech with the introduction and conclusion removed. Choose from any of the speeches in the *Instructor's Manual to accompany The Art of Public Speaking*, 8th ed. "Edible Insects" is a good one because it inspires a lot of imagination. Have each group write an introduction and conclusion for the speech following the criteria for effective introductions and conclusions presented in Chapter 9. Students can assume the audience is their own class, or the instructor can change audiences for each group. Each group should write out the introduction and conclusion and post it on the discussion board for all to read.

Course Design Principle: Fulfills Principle #3 because it is assigned for groups or partners and requires considerable collaboration. It also requires elements from Principle #4, critical evaluation and reflection.

Assignment Design Characteristics: #1-#5

Teaching Tips: Reading these postings can be very entertaining. Be sure you have communicated exactly how you will grade both the introduction and conclusion. You can extend the value of the assignment by asking each group to post a collaborative evaluation of another group's work using the criteria suggested in the text. Again, you should be explicit about how you will grade these submissions.

Chapter Eleven – Language

"Got Style?"

Objective(s): Students should be able to identify major linguistic devices and explain to what effect they are used in a speech.

Source material: Based on "Exercises for Critical Thinking" #4 in *The Art of Public Speaking*, 8th ed., p. 290.

Description: Ask students to view "A Question of Culture" from the Lucas Student CD-ROM. Then have them read the manuscript of the speech in the "Speeches for Analysis and Discussion" appendix at the end of *The Art of Public Speaking*, 8th ed. Instruct them to answer the following questions:

1. Identify three or more linguistic devices (like metaphor, repetition, etc.) used by the speaker. Quote and label them, and explain how they make his speech clear, vivid and appropriate.
2. What is the linguistic device that the speaker uses most often? Quote phrases that are examples of this major linguistic device.
3. How does this device affect his message and the ultimate success of his speech?
4. What is "style," as it relates to oral language?

Course Design Principle: Fulfills Principles #4 and #5, because it requires students to analyze language use in a speech by both listening to and reading it.

Assignment Design Characteristics: #1-#4

Teaching Tips: This exercise is quite straightforward and easy to grade by assigning points for the answers. The answer to question #4 is not found in the chapter per se, and you might warn the students that they may have to consult another source. It is a challenge for many students to relate language use to the concept of style in speaking. However, the answer to the question makes a logical transition to Chapter Twelve.

Chapter Twelve – Delivery

"Compare and Contrast Delivery Styles"

Objective(s): The student should be able to identify and explain the major characteristics of effective speech delivery.

Source material: Based on "Exercises for Critical Thinking" #3 in *The Art of Public Speaking*, 8th ed., p. 318.

Description: After assigning the students to read Chapter Twelve, choose two speeches from the Lucas Student CD-ROM that display obvious differences in delivery style. Good choices are "Question of Culture" and "Dying To Be Thin." Ask the students to view the speeches and write a paper comparing and contrasting the delivery styles of the speakers. Students should base their answers on the following questions:

1. In each case, what is the type of speech being given and what is the occasion?
2. Compare and contrast the delivery style of each speaker, discussing specifically how the following items enhanced or detracted from the speaker's message:
   - Method of delivery
   - Vocal variety (rate, pitch, pronunciation, articulation, volume, etc.)
   - Non-verbal aspects of communication (body language)
3. Explain which speech you enjoyed most and why, referring to factors you learned in Chapter 12 about good delivery.

Course Design Principle(s): Fulfills Principles #4, for critical reflection, and #5, for incorporation of different media.

Assignment Design Characteristics: #1-4

Teaching Tips: Because this exercise requires students to directly apply concepts to real-world situations, they tend to enjoy it. It puts them in the teacher's place and gives them the opportunity to make objective observations and evaluate the speakers based on sound principle. Consequently, their answers make for interesting reading. You will want to make clear how you will grade the assignment and whether you expect a formal essay or paper and of what length. Another option is to send students out to evaluate "live" speakers outside the classroom and follow the same assignment strategy above.

Chapter Thirteen – Using Visual Aids; Appendix: Using PowerPoint
Chapter Fourteen – Speaking to Inform
"Need Pix?"

Objective(s): Students should be able to determine when a visual aid should be used and why. Students should be able to decide what kind of visual aid to prepare and how and at what point in the speech to use it. Students should be able to organize ideas concisely so that listeners can easily grasp and recall the content.

Source material: Based on "Applying the Power of Public Speaking" in *The Art of Public Speaking*, p. 390, and "A Critical Thinking Approach to the Use of Visual Aids," by Mary Ann Danielson in *Selections from The Speech Communication Teacher, 1994-1996*, pp. 64-65.

Description: This is a big project that requires some time and thought. It can be done as an individual or in a collaborative mode, like small groups or partnerships. Referring to the scenario of the coffeehouse manager's speech preparation in Chapter 14's "Applying the Power of Public Speaking" (p. 390), ask your students to answer and do the following:

1. Write an essay explaining the challenges the manager faces in his speech preparation with regard to his audience and content. State specifically:
    - How you, as the manager, will organize your main points more concisely.
    - Your specific purpose and central idea.
    - Your method of organization.
    - Anything else the manager should take into consideration with regard to content and audience.

2. Continue your essay and address the following:
    - Should a visual aid be used in this scenario? Why or why not? (State what factors influenced your decision.)
    - If a visual should be used, what form should it take (transparency, objects, computer-generated graphics or content, etc.)? Describe your visual(s) in detail. If you opt for a transparency or PowerPoint slide, state precisely what you will put on the slide (what graphic, bulleted points, etc.).
    - At what point in the speech should the visual(s) be used?
    - What do you hope will be the specific response of your audience when you use the visual aids?

Course Design Principle(s): The exercise will challenge critical thinking skills (Principle #4), require collaboration if assigned as a group or partnership project (Principle #3), and can incorporate alternative media as an option (Principle #5).

Assignment Design Characteristics: #1-#5

Teaching Tips: Although this project seems rather complicated, at this point students should be ready to synthesize material and apply it to real-life situations. The unique part of the assignment asks students to determine whether there is a real need for a visual and what the visual is expected to accomplish in light of the speaker's stated purpose. So many times students are merely required to use a visual and are not forced to consider why, from a pedagogical standpoint, they are doing so. You may want to assign this as a formal paper, although it could be done with more brevity to ease the grading time. Given the reflective nature of the second part, involving the need for visuals, you may find that you receive more thoughtful answers if you assign an essay.

One more level of complexity may be added to this project by requiring students to send you a PowerPoint slide of an actual visual they design for the speech.

Chapter Fifteen – Speaking to Persuade

"Monroe Analyzed"

"Monroe Synthesized"

Monroe Analyzed

Objective: Students should be able to identify the five steps of Monroe's Motivated Sequence.

Source material: Based on "Exercises for Critical Thinking" #6 in *The Art of Public Speaking,* 8th ed., p. 424.

Course Design Principle(s): Fulfills Principle #4, critical reflection with analysis.

Assignment Design Characteristics: #1, #2 and #4

Description: Students should analyze the manuscript for a persuasive speech that uses Monroe's Motivated Sequence, such as "The Ultimate Gift" by Jennifer Conard. Ask students to write an analysis that focuses on how the speaker develops each step of the sequence (attention, need, satisfaction, visualization and action). Have students identify where each step of the sequence occurs in the speech and explain how the persuasive appeal of the speech builds from step to step.

Teaching Tips: You may opt to make the speech available electronically as a Word document. Students can insert their labels and comments in a contrasting color. If you assign the activity in this fashion, be sure to explain how you want the students to insert their comments and exactly what types of comments you will look for in each entry. Also, tell them how you will grade their entries. For example, you might offer the following instructions:

1. Read and study the manuscript.
2. Divide the manuscript by the parts of Monroe's Motivated Sequence by inserting a label before the paragraph(s) containing that part. For example, the label "ATTENTION" would go on the line above the paragraph(s) containing the Attention step.
3. Labels are worth one point each.
4. Between parts of the sequence (as determined by labels), comment on the function of that part in light of its persuasive appeal and how it is developed (5 points each).
5. Post document as homework. Use a dark, contrasting color (dark blue, purple, dark green) in boldface to display your labels and analysis.

Should you not want to offer this activity electronically, have students study, analyze and submit this as a homework essay.

Monroe Synthesized

Objective: Students should be able to implement the five steps of Monroe's Motivated Sequence.

Source material: Based on "Additional Exercises and Activities" #4 in the *Instructor's Manual* to accompany *The Art of Public Speaking*, 8th ed.

Description: Divide students into groups of five, assigning each member to a step of Monroe's Motivated Sequence. If there is an odd man out, pair him or her with a group member who is assigned to the Need, Satisfaction or Visualization steps. If you are left with a four-man team, assign one person to both the Attention and the Action steps.

Have each group prepare as if they were giving a one-minute speech with the specific purpose, "To persuade my audience that all students should take a course in public speaking." The speech must be organized according to Monroe's Motivated Sequence. Each group should assign one person to write each part of the sequence, discuss their work online or by other means, and then post their submissions on the forum as a short manuscript speech. Each part should be labeled.

Course Design Principle(s): Fulfills Principle #3, for student collaboration; #4, as above with synthesis; and #5, for creative use of media (forum) to post the speech.

Assignment Design Characteristics: #1-#5 and #7

Teaching Tips: If you use your forum for displaying these "speeches," you may want to suggest that each part be no longer than a paragraph of a certain word length. Or you may instruct groups to submit their speech as a single Word document, which you could then make available for the other groups to read. You may assign different specific purposes to each group if you wish. Be sure to reward those who think to use source citations, even if they are from the textbook.

Chapter Sixteen – Methods of Persuasion

"Virtual Debate"

Objective: Students should be able to use evidence effectively when supporting a controversial position.

Source material: Based on "Debate as the Key to Teaching Persuasion Skills" by Kimberly A. Powell in *Selections from The Speech Communication Teacher, 1994-1996*, p. 83-84. Formatted with the help of Table Two, "Sequence of Steps in a Virtual Debate," in "Moderating Learner-Centered E-Learning," by Curtis J. Bonk, et al., p. 28.

Description: In order to execute this assignment effectively, the courseware should have a forum that is easy for the students and instructor to navigate and utilize. Your directions and method of assessment should be made very clear to the students. Your directions to the students should be based on the following steps for a virtual debate:

1. Divide the class into groups of four.
2. Groups choose from a list of topics, such as abortion, capital punishment, euthanasia, legalization of marijuana, etc.
3. The group writes a claim or a position statement, such as "Abortion should be made illegal in the United States."
4. Students within the groups choose sides. Two people in the group should research and argue the negative, and the other pair, the affirmative, regardless of personal position.
5. Student pairs do research on their position and furnish at least three sources.
6. In the forum, each critic and defender pair post their initial position statements. Put the claim or position in the message box's subject line with "affirmative" or "negative."
7. ALL students review the initial position statements of each group.
8. Each student should reply to at least two position statements from other groups with comments or questions that challenge the position.
9. Each pair should rebut the opposing argument in the group.
10. Based on a review of all statements, comments and questions, all students should formulate a personal position statement on a topic outside their group.
11. Each student should post a personal position statement in a private forum or to the instructor by alternate means.

Course Design Principle(s): This is an ultra-sophisticated online activity and incorporates all the Principles #1-#5. It involves analysis, synthesis, research, critical reflection and evaluation, sharing, student-student collaboration, student-teacher interaction (teacher in the role of moderator, weaver or adviser), and extensive use of the forum platform.

Assignment Design Characteristics: #1-#5 and #7

Teaching Tips: This exercise requires considerable planning, clear direction and thoughtful assessment. It is very beneficial to the students because they see how evidence is used to support a claim and how their peers can challenge it. You should structure the debate so that students have time to research responses to these challenges, allowing a day or two between the initial postings, the responses, and the submission of final responses and personal position statements. Your role is one of supervision, moderating, weaving, or adding thoughts and commentary where needed. Students love the challenge of online confrontation and learn to be succinct in their statements while supporting them with credible sources. By reviewing the evidence and formulating their own positions on a topic, they also learn that there is more to an argument than just one's opinion.

Chapter Seventeen – Speaking on Special Occasions
"Speakers' Séance"

Objective(s): Students should be able to apply the guidelines for an effective speech of introduction.

Source material: Based on the annotated "Speech Assignment" in the margin of the Annotated Instructor's Edition of *The Art of Public Speaking*, 8th ed., p. 467; and the Electronic Séance activity by Curtis J. Bonk in workshop entitled "Mediating Discussion and Mentoring Students for Interactive Online Learning" at IUPUI.

Description: You can call this the Speaker's Séance, Meet the Dead, or any other creative title that inspires the imaginations of your students. Tell students that they should imagine themselves being able to invite any well-known *deceased* person to speak to the class on a topic of the student's choice. Instruct students to write a researched introduction of this person, as if that person were really coming to class, using the guidelines for a proper introduction from Chapter 17. Suggest that the students model their introduction on the sample in the chapter. The speech should not to exceed 250 words (or whatever length you believe is appropriate). Students should post their speech in the discussion forum with the name of the deceased in the subject line.

Course Design Principle(s): Fulfills Principle #1 because this exercise applies course content to a real-world activity, and #5, because it uses the discussion platform to provide an electronic "speaking" venue.

Assignment Design Characteristics: #1-5 and 7

Teaching Tips: You should require students to cite their sources, but not within the speech unless appropriate. I suggest limiting the length of the introduction for ease of reading and grading. Force the students to read the postings by having them "vote" for the speaker they would invite to class by replying positively to that speaker's introduction.

Chapter Eighteen – Speaking in Small Groups
"Decisions Through Reflective Thinking"

It should be noted here that presenting group discussions/problem-solving sessions online is quite possible, but requires extensive structuring and planning. Refer to the Murray, Wakley, Klemm, and Bonk ("Moderator Centered E-Learning") articles for extensive research of online discussion techniques, structure and assessment. Although full-blown discussions as they are described in these resources are beyond the scope of this document, preparation for online group decision-making discussions can be made with the following assignment.

Objective: Students should be able to identify the five stages of the reflective-thinking process and discuss the major tasks of the group at this stage.

Source material: Based on "Exercises for Critical Thinking" #3 in *The Art of Public Speaking*, 8th ed., p. 499.

Course Design Principle(s): Fulfills Principle #4, for critical reflection on a real-world problem.

Assignment Design Characteristics: #1, #2 and #4

Description: Ask students to identify a relatively important decision they have made in the last year or two. Suggest such things as getting engaged or married; buying a car, house, or similar big-ticket item; choosing a college; or choosing, changing or quitting a job or career. Ask students to reconstruct how they reached that decision. Then, ask them to make their decision again, using the reflective-thinking method. Tell them to map out exactly what they would do at each stage of the method. Did they still reach the same decision? If not, did they think that the reflective-thinking method would have led them to a better decision in the first place?

Teaching Tips: This is a basic essay or formal paper posted online as a homework assignment. It creates the opportunity for deep thought and practical reflection, and as such, requires substantial instructor reading and evaluation time. You should devise some kind of scoring rubric for grading and describe it clearly to the students. This exercise is worthwhile because it requires the students to apply a time-tested technique to a real-life problem of their own. Thinking through the procedure in this way can prepare students for live group decision-making sessions, should you have time for them in an online class that requires some face-to-face meetings.

Teaching Tips and Resources

Included in this section:
- The impact of class size on teaching on learning
- Survival tips for teaching online
- Course management information from a syllabus by Nan Peck
- Sample distance-learning survey questions
- Excerpt from a course schedule by Jennifer Cochrane
- Oral assignments

The Impact of Class Size on Teaching and Learning

Class size is always an issue, and the online class is no exception. For administrators, class size boils down to economics and student credit hours. For teachers, it is the number of students, lectures to prepare and deliver, and the amount of student work to read and grade. For traditional speech teachers, the issues are the same, with the addition of a set number of speeches that must be listened to in a semester or quarter. For online teachers, who teach by facilitating and commenting on the discussion postings, homework, oral speeches and e-mails of every student and listening to oral presentations, whether on tape or in person, the issue may be one of quality.

The issue is not only whether online teaching takes more time than in a traditional class, but that the *quality of online teaching and learning decreases exponentially as the class size increases*. It is important that online teachers have class sizes that reasonably fit the pedagogy necessary for successful online teaching and learning. As mentioned earlier, this pedagogy requires frequent, timely and personable online presence.

Dan Hobbs' review of the literature (63) emphasizes that collaborative discussion activities enhance student learning. He also makes the point that student perception of learning quality increases proportionally with active faculty involvement. If collaboration among students and frequent student-teacher interactions are built into your Web courses (Course Design Principles 2 and 3), it follows that you will have to be accessible on a frequent basis in order to affect student learning significantly. This may require hours of sitting in front of a computer, responding to the needs of every one of your students.

It is important that you keep track of your time (some courseware automatically times your logging in and out), so that you can explain the necessary time commitments to your administrators, if it is necessary to lobby for a smaller class size. Emphasize, too, that your online presence is the "human touch" that is necessary to decrease the psychological distance, engage the students, and retain them in your class.

Depending on the rigor of your course, a class size of twenty is excellent. Twenty-five is possible, but slows down teacher response time considerably. If your communication *is* your pedagogy, you will need to show evidence of what class size allows you to be the most effective. Don't forget to add the time it takes to you to listen to speeches. Optimum class size may take a number of semesters to determine.

Survival Tips for Teaching Online

If you are new to online teaching and learning, please consider the following:

- Pay very strict attention to the number of exercises and assignments you generate to satisfy your course learning outcomes. It is so easy to want to assign too much. Be conservative at first; you can always add assignments later.

- Keep in mind that the first few days online are very crucial. From the outset, your challenge is to decrease the psychological distance in your class and foster interaction. Pay close attention to how you word your messages, making sure they are frequent, encouraging and warm. Do not forget to begin your class with a "first day" exercise like "Cyber Café," "Good Speaker/Bad Speaker" or both, so that your students get a sense that they are part of a group. Also, you can send your class on an online scavenger hunt, asking them to find and post key course management information, such as "What is the policy for homework deadlines?" "How does the instructor define 'attendance'?" "How many speeches are required?" etc. This not only helps the students become familiar with the course information, but also forces them to share the information on the discussion board. It cannot be said often enough that interaction among the class members can be the key to retention. "First day" experiences such as these get students off on the right foot.

- Be firm about deadlines for homework submission. If you aren't, students will be sending in course assignments at times inappropriate to their skill-building or informational needs. More to the point, you will be grading assignments out of order and find it difficult to keep everyone's progress straight. If your students do not meet your deadlines well, try not giving credit for late assignments. On the positive side, this helps students discipline themselves in time management. Offer to review the assignment even if you don't give them credit. Then offer opportunities during the course for extra credit points that will ease the pain of your late assignment policy.

- If you have strict homework deadlines, you can grade the same assignment all at once. This helps you manage your time and will give you a better sense of the students' understanding of the concepts.

- Communicate to your students when you will be returning the graded assignments. This will reduce the number of e-mails you will receive with regard to the posting of grades, etc.

- When you communicate with your students, resist the urge to answer their queries without using their names. "Dear Kristin" is warmer than not using a name in the message. Also, discipline yourself to be very personable in those e-mail messages, as well as in your homework evaluations, etc. Your responses, whatever form they take, *are* your teaching. They take the place of the interpersonal communication found in a traditional class, minus the non-verbals. In a sense, you have to make up for the lack of personal presence with very well-crafted written reflections of you and your ideas.

- It is helpful, after speeches or large projects, to summarize what you think the students should have learned up to that point. Communicate your sense of how you think the students have progressed corporately. This will help give students the "big picture" of their learning and can be very encouraging as well as challenging.

- If you intend to do a virtual debate or a threaded discussion, read up on each of these types of experiences. Your role will change to weaver, moderator and facilitator, as opposed to "teacher." Your consistent online presence will be needed. Explaining and grading threaded discussions and debates will be a challenge. See the Suggested Readings section for relevant journal articles and book chapters on the subject of online discussions.

- Have a flexible attitude about technological crises, but be consistent and fair. Make sure you have back-up plans for receiving homework online.

- Be fair to yourself and your family when you take on the online teaching challenge. If you can, decide when, where and how often you will do your online grading and communicating work. For example, you might decide to grade homework only at the office, and check e-mail only once at home. It is important to balance your personal time with course time, or you will find yourself a slave to the class.

Sample Course Management Information

The following is an example of course management information from part of a syllabus by Nan Peck at Northern Virginia Community College, Extended Learning Institute (ELI) in Annandale, Virginia. Although the syllabus is not reproduced in its entirety, this excerpt is offered as a way to organize and format information that is relevant to an online course. Note the convenient syllabus table of contents, below, and the subsequent "chunking" of information in the following pages. The visual framework makes the information easy to find, read, navigate and print. Notice also the abundant use of white space, bulleted listings and succinct narrative.

Inside this *Syllabus*:

Refund and Withdrawal Form 2

Getting Started 6

Course-Specific Information 6
Course Summary 6
Course Objectives..6
Course Materials 6
Grading Scale 6
Class Assignments Schedule 7

Using Technologies..8
Internet...10
TV/Video Programs..11
Voice Mail Technology 12
For Students Who Are Imprisoned or Homebound Only...13

ELI Policies and Procedures..12
Academic Dishonesty 12
Examinations 12
Limited Services During Holidays 12
NVCC ID Cards..12
Parking on Campus 12
Submission of Work 12

ELI Voice Mail Information Line..15

Campus Learning Resource Centers and Bookstores 16

Extended Learning Institute Office and Mailing Addresses...16

Getting Started

Welcome to SPD 100: PRINCIPLES OF PUBLIC SPEAKING, and to ELI! This *Syllabus* provides information on your course requirements, required books and materials, assignments and examinations, and policies governing your enrollment. Be sure to read this *Syllabus* carefully. While you have some flexibility in how you complete this course, your enrollment in this course starts immediately, so you need to get started now. The ELI faculty and staff are ready to assist you, but it is ultimately your responsibility to complete your course.

For questions not answered in this *Syllabus* or your *Course Guide,* call:

- ☎ The **ELI Hotline**, (703) 323-3347, to speak to a staff person between 8:30 a.m. and 5:00 p.m., Monday through Friday, or to speak to your instructor during his or her office hours. If you are hearing impaired, call the V/TDD number, (703) 323-3717, and leave a message. The **toll free** number is 1-800-627-5443.

- ☎ The **ELI Voice Mail Service**, (703) 323-3713, to leave messages or to receive additional information. For your instructor, dial the number, select Option 2 (*visit other mailboxes*), then enter **0826** when prompted. For other information, please see the next to the last page of this *Syllabus* for directions.

Course-Specific Information

Course Summary

SPD 100 is designed to increase your knowledge and awareness of the theory and principles of public address. You will be given several opportunities to develop your confidence as a public speaker as well as to organize, develop and listen to spoken discourse.

Course Objectives

Upon successful completion of SPD 100, you should be able to demonstrate an increased understanding of and appreciation for the communication process as it relates to speaker and audience interactions. We seek to develop speaking and listening skills for effective speech composition and delivery. Upon successful completion of this course, you will demonstrate:

- development of critical insight for being able to judge spoken discourse
- development of an appreciation for how spoken communication is used to critically examine facts, values and policies
- development of a respect for the ethical codes that govern discourse: tolerance for reasonable differences of opinion; the preference for civility; the willingness to put evidence and arguments to tests of rationality; and the fostering of interpersonal values that open and maintain channels of communication.

As with any speech communication course, upon successful completion you should be able to:

- report increased self-confidence
- express your ideas with verbal fluency
- apply knowledge of nonverbal communication in sending and receiving messages
- demonstrate critical thinking skills in sending and receiving messages
- demonstrate organizational skills
- adapt messages and behaviors to different communication contexts
- employ listening and responding skills adapted to different communication contexts
- demonstrate an understanding and respect for cultural and social diversity

Course Materials

The textbooks and other materials for this course are:

1. Your textbook, authored by Stephen E. Lucas and entitled, *The Art of Public Speaking*. 7th edition. New York: McGraw-Hill, Inc., 2001.
2. The *Course Guide* for SPD 100.

You can buy these at the campus bookstores listed on the last page of this *Syllabus* or you may call 1-888-744-7839 to order them by mail. Buying your books by mail takes time, so do it immediately. Before traveling to the bookstore, you may call ahead to confirm that your books are in stock. Also, take your *Syllabus* with you when purchasing your textbooks and *Course Guide*, so you are sure to get the right books for your course. Each bookstore has a special section for ELI books. If you don't see what you need, be sure to ask bookstore personnel for assistance.

Grading Scale

The course grading criteria are listed below. Please keep a personal record of all your grades so that you can compute your own course grade. Final grades will be based on the following scale:

> Class Participation (0-100 points)
> Two Written Examinations (0-50 points each = 100 points)
> Graded Speeches (0-200 points)
>> Personal Narrative (0-50 points)
>> Demonstration Speech (0-50 points)
>> Persuasive Talk (0-100 points)
> Two Speech Preparation Outlines (0-25 points each = 50 points)
> Self-Critique of Speech (0-50 points)

Consult your *Course Guide*, pages 4-5, for descriptions of these assignments.

To calculate your final grade, you will be assigned the following: 450-500 points = A

400-449 points = B
300-399 points = C
250-299 points = D
0-249 points = F

Please keep a personal record of all your grades so that you can compute your own course grade.

If you do not withdraw and do not finish your course assignments, you will receive a grade based upon the work you have submitted. Usually, this grade is an "F."

Class Meetings

There will be four MANDATORY CLASS MEETINGS for this course:
    Wednesday, Feb. 6, 2002, 7:00-10:00 p.m.
    Wednesday, March 6, 2002, 7:00-10:00 p.m.
    Wednesday, April 10, 2002, 7:00-10:00 p.m.
    Wednesday, May 8, 2002, 7:00-10:00 p.m.

All meetings will take place at the Extended Learning Institute, 8000 Forbes Place, Springfield, VA. If you will be unable to attend these sessions, complete the Refund and Withdrawal Form (page 2) *before* your refund date (see front cover of this *Syllabus*). See the last page for directions to ELI.

You will be expected to present your speeches and provide your classmates with feedback on their talks as well. Expect 20-30 students at these sessions. Your instructor will provide you with immediate written feedback (and a graded evaluation), and a camcorder will be set up to record your presentation. Be sure to bring your videotape (VHS format). This is your opportunity to meet your classmates and your instructor and to conduct audience analysis for your presentations.

Sample Distance Learning Survey

This two-part questionnaire is required of every student who wants to take the online basic speech course at IUPUI(Comm. R110). Although it is not a predictor of success, it causes the potential students to begin thinking about their learning style, lifestyle and technical expertise. The first ten questions deal with learning and life; the last ten deal with technical expertise. Results of the survey are sent to both the student and the instructor and used to determine whether learning in an online environment is the best way for the student to take the course.

This survey has been adapted from the Readiness Index for Learning Online, created by Serena Novosel, M.S., of the Indiana University School of Nursing in Indianapolis, IN.

R110 ONLINE READINESS SURVEY

Choose the answers that best describe you. Answer ALL of the questions and submit the survey for scoring. Wait for your score and the explanation of how to interpret it.
Name:
E-mail:

Part I: Learning Styles

1. Face-to-face interaction with the instructor is:
    ☐   An important part of the learning process for me.
    ☐   Somewhat important to me.
    ☐   Not necessary for my success.

2. Participating in face-to-face classroom discussion is:
    ☐   A central part of my learning style.
    ☐   Somewhat important to me.
    ☐   Not so important to me.

3. I consider my reading skills to be:
    ☐   Excellent. I rarely need help to understand the text.
    ☐   Good. Occasionally I need help to understand the text.
    ☐   Fair. I frequently need help to understand the text.

4. Do you like to work independently?
    ☐   Sometimes, but I like to have help available when I need it.
    ☐   Yes, I enjoy figuring things out for myself.
    ☐   No, I prefer a structured classroom to do my best.

5. In what type of classroom setting do you learn best?
    ☐   Independent study—self-taught learning.
    ☐   Student-centered learning—work on my own, but ask questions as needed.
    ☐   Teacher-directed environment—all details explained.

6. Face-to-face interaction and feedback from other classmates is:
    ☐   Important to me.
    ☐   Somewhat important to me.
    ☐   Not so important to me.

7. Considering my professional and personal schedule, the amount of time I have to work on my online course is:
    ☐   More than for a class on campus.
    ☐   The same as for a class on campus.
    ☐   Less than for a class on campus.

8. What is your expectation about the amount of time it will take to complete this course online?
   - ☐ An online course takes the same amount of time as a course taught on site.
   - ☐ An online course takes less time than a course taught on site.
   - ☐ An online course takes more time than a course taught on site.

9. How would you describe your ability to assess your own progress?
   - ☐ Excellent. I am able to accurately judge my progress in a course and keep track of my grades.
   - ☐ Good. I am usually able to recognize my strengths and weaknesses, and I am generally proactive about keeping track of my grades.
   - ☐ I am often confused about my progress in my classes. I require frequent feedback from my instructor.

10. Although many courses are delivered solely online, R110 Online requires that you come to campus three Saturdays (check Insite for dates).
    - ☐ I can attend all three dates.
    - ☐ I can attend some of the dates.
    - ☐ I am unable to attend any of the dates.

Part II: Technical Expertise

1. How would you describe your experience with e-mail?
   - ☐ Extensive—I use e-mail daily and am able to attach and open files.
   - ☐ Moderate—I have used e-mail periodically. I can paste text from a word-processing document into an e-mail message.
   - ☐ Minimal—I rarely use e-mail.

2. What is your comfort level with computers?
   - ☐ Expert—I can run applications, install software, download and upload files, and do minor troubleshooting when needed.
   - ☐ Intermediate—I can use word-processing software, and sometimes need assistance with applications, software and file management.
   - ☐ Beginner—I am uncomfortable with computers and have little experience using them.

3. Which answer best represents your computer access at the present time?
   - ☐ I will need to use a computer at a facility away from my primary place of residence, but I do not know where one is located or what hours they are open.
   - ☐ I will need to use a computer at a facility away from my primary place of residence, but I know where at least two computers are located for my use and their hours of operation.
   - ☐ I have an Internet-ready computer available to me either where I live or work, any time I need it.

4. How would you describe your feelings when asked to learn a new software package?
   - ☐ Scared—I prefer a lot of one-on-one assistance to learn new applications or technologies.
   - ☐ Nervous—I may need a little help, but I think I can learn.
   - ☐ Excited—I love to learn new things.

5. When confronted with a technology that is new to me:
   - ☐ I jump in eagerly.
   - ☐ I tread cautiously. I am somewhat apprehensive but try anyway.
   - ☐ I pull back. I try to delay using new technologies if I can help it.

6. WordPerfect and Microsoft Word are examples of:
   - ☐ Search engines.
   - ☐ Word-processing software.
   - ☐ Web browsers.

7. Netscape and Internet Explorer are examples of:
   - ☐ Search engines.
   - ☐ Word-processing software.
   - ☐ Web browsers.

8. My experience with the World Wide Web is:
   - ☐ Extensive—I use the Web daily to do research and surf for fun. I feel very comfortable with it.
   - ☐ Moderate—I have used Web search engines periodically, but I have mostly used the Web for fun.
   - ☐ Minimal—I rarely use the Web. I can search for information with assistance.

9. HotBot, Infoseek and Yahoo! are examples of:
   - ☐ Search engines.
   - ☐ Word-processing software.
   - ☐ Web browsers.

10. When online research is appropriate:
   - ☐ I avoid researching online if I can help it.
   - ☐ I sometimes research online.
   - ☐ I feel comfortable conducting research online.

11. If I experience difficulty gaining access to IUPUI computer resources:
   - ☐ I am familiar with IUPUI support resources and feel confident that I could get help.
   - ☐ I am somewhat familiar with IUPUI support resources, but may need help locating them.
   - ☐ I am not familiar with IUPUI support resources, and not sure how I would obtain help.

Sample Course Schedule

Figure 9 represents the Course Schedule, Unit One , and Week One of the fifteen-week public speaking course at IUPUI using *The Art of Public Speaking*. This is taken from Communication R110 online and was developed by Jennifer Cochrane. The class is presented online within the Indiana in-house learning environment, "Oncourse." Note the frequent chunking of information and the abundant white space. The schedule of unitized contents, which includes Unit One and Week One, are displayed as separate pages on the Web even though they do not appear that way in print below. Organizational features include unitizing of course content and monthly graphic calendars (not shown) with deadlines noted.

Figure 9
Sample Course Schedule

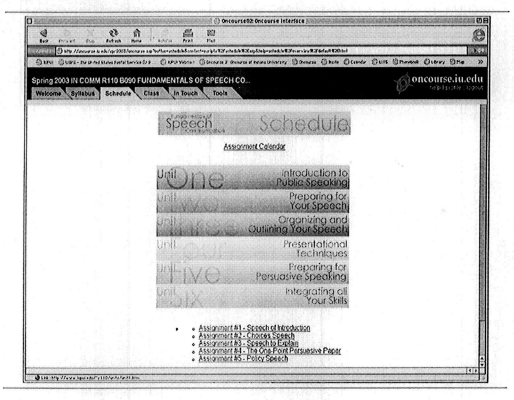

Unit 1 -Introduction to Public Speaking

Questions answered in this unit:

1. What is public speaking? (Isn't this something I do everyday?)
2. How does good listening relate to good speaking? (Can't I give a speech without being a good listener?)
3. What is ethical listening? What is ethical speaking? (What's "ethical" about listening?)
4. What do I have to know about my audience in order to craft a good speech? (You mean that I have to do an "analysis" of my audiences?)
5. Who are the individuals who comprise my R110 audience? (How will I find out enough about my classmates to give an interesting speech?)

Work Requirements:

- Read four chapters in text
- Two class discussions
- Three homework assignments
- One speech (plus one speech outline)

Weekly Outline:

Week One - January 13-19

Week Two - January 20-26

Week Three - January 27-February 2

Unit 1 - Week One - January 13-19- Introduction to Public Speaking

Reading Assignments: Read Chapters 1,2 and 3 along with CD-ROM clips. Try all study questions and reflect on your answers. (Estimated work time: Chapter 1, 1.5 hours; Chapter 2, 1.5 hours; Chapter 3, 1 hour)

Forum Assignments:

Forum Homework #1-1- "Effective/Ineffective Speaker" on #2 and #3, p. 28; Post by midnight, Wednesday, January 15.

Forum Homework #1-2 -"Felicia Robinson: What should she do?" on #1, p. 51; Post response by midnight, Thursday, January 16.

Homework #1-3: View the *Cryonics* speech on the Lucas Student CD-ROM, Disk Two. Take notes by using the keyword method (as described in the chapter) and post as homework online no later than midnight, Saturday, January 18. (Estimated time: 45 minutes)

Task List For Project Management

This is a task checklist to help you manage your course development. The times allotted for task completion are estimated and assume that you have other classes and projects that occupy your time while you are trying to develop your online course. However, if you manage to get release time to complete your course development, you can easily cut the suggested times by one third to one half. Also, if you are especially technically experienced, the time it takes you to actually put your course into a Web-based framework may decrease significantly. Conversely, if you are new to instructional design and have little technical expertise, you may wish to take as much as one year to develop your course.

ESTIMATED TIME	TASK(S)	COMPLETED
2 Months	**Locate Resources**	☐
	Find and study other online courses.	☐
	Talk to online course teachers and students.	☐
	Ask for release time or write for grant.	☐
	Locate/take course-development seminars.	☐
	Locate/consult local instructional designers.	☐
	Locate/consult local technical designers.	☐
	Locate online development documents.	☐
	Review current literature re: online pedagogy.	☐
	Analyze Student Base	☐
	Who will take your course?	☐
	What geographical area?	☐
	Educational, social characteristics of base?	☐
	Technical expertise of base?	☐
	What is the purpose for taking your course?	☐
	Analyze Institutional Expectations	☐
	Is your course a general education requirement?	☐
	Will it transfer as such to other institutions?	☐
	Will it transfer as such to other units?	☐
	Subject to open enrollment?	☐
	Are students selected into your course?	☐
	How are students selected?	☐
	Are there prerequisites?	☐
1 Month	**Articulate or Create Course Objectives**	☐
	Articulate objective for basic course.	☐
	Articulate learning outcomes for content units.	☐
	Articulate learning outcomes for oral assignments.	☐
	Assess Objectives/Outcomes for Online Delivery	☐
	What parts of course must be face-to-face?	☐
	If totally online, how are speaking opportunities created?	☐
	What parts of the course can be delivered online?	☐
4 months	**Create Activities for Online Delivery**	☐
	Become familiar with Web characteristics.*	☐
	Become familiar with courseware features.	☐
	Generate activities, exercises that satisfy outcomes.**	☐
	Rethink/retool exercises for active Web learning.***	☐

ESTIMATED TIME	TASK(S)	COMPLETED
	Make sure exercises prepare students for oral assignments.	☐
	Develop schedule for content-based assignments.	☐
	Add oral assignments to schedule.	☐
	Create and Schedule Internal Assessment Tools.	☐
	Embed self and peer evaluations in oral speech work.	☐
	Create and schedule testing tools.	☐
	Assign reflective forums or papers. (What did I learn?)	☐
	Schedule outside speaker evaluations.	☐
	Use CD-ROM speeches for student analysis.	☐
	Schedule institutional assessment tool.	☐
	Generate Course Management Information	☐
	Locate sample course information from online courses.	☐
	Organize information into logical chunks.	☐
	Make information easy-to-find, navigate and print.	☐
	Keep general information separate from course assignments.	☐
2 Months	**Prepare Online Environment**	☐
	Create website or activate online courseware…	☐
	Learn Web authoring tools.	☐
	Load course information (syllabus, schedule).	☐
	Create visually pleasing pages, easy to print and navigate.	
Up to 1 Month	**Check Course Page/Courseware Functions** With the help of others:	☐
	Check spelling.	☐
	Check links.	☐
	Check downloads.	☐
	Check dates.	☐
	Perform general tweaking.	☐
	Pilot or Implement Course	☐
	Ask students to help you de-bug the pages throughout the duration of the class.	☐
	Make changes immediately as you become aware of them.	☐

* See "Changing the Web Environment into a Learning Environment", p.____.
** See Compendium of Online Activities, p. ____, for ideas.
*** See Assignment Design Characteristics, p. ____.

Oral Assignments

The Online Learning Environment Should Prepare Students for Oral Assignments

There are as many combinations and configurations of oral assignments as there are instructors and universities. Some of you will evaluate speeches on tape; others, in person. Student populations will be unique, as will the geographical areas from which they come. Even though the type of online course and the student population characteristics will affect your course design, it is beyond the scope of this supplement to dictate what should or should not be included as oral assignments. However, it is best practice to begin with oral assignments that focus on very basic skills (like a speech of self-introduction) and then progress sequentially to more sophisticated speeches that require in-depth strategy, logic and audience awareness (like a persuasive speech of policy). The reading assignments, activities and exercises that the students complete online prior to each speech should bring them to the level of competency necessary to prepare and perform that speech.

The Online Learning Environment Should Support Oral Experiences

Online teachers may find that getting students prepared for and through the first speech is a huge hurdle. Generally, if students can get through that first speech, they tend to stay in the class. If you teach a course with limited in-class time, your first meeting face-to-face with your class may be for giving the first speech. It is very easy, under these circumstances, for the students *not* to want to come. And sometimes they don't. Attrition can be very high during the early parts of the course.

You can do several things to minimize the anxiety and resultant attrition. At IUPUI, where only three face-to-face class meetings are allowed, the very first speech is one of self-introduction. Instead of meeting face-to-face to hear these short speeches, students tape their self-introductions on audiocassette tape and send it, along with a picture, to be digitized and posted on a Web page. Some students send their speeches and pictures in digital files. The entire class is required to access all the speeches, listen to them while looking at the speaker's picture, and take notes on the demographic characteristics revealed by the speakers. Just hearing the voices of all their classmates and being able to focus on audience characteristics and commonalities is a great relief to the students. As they do the required class audience analysis assignment, they find they are grateful for the chance to connect with their classmates in this way. This taped assignment, in addition to a first-day social activity in a "cyber café" (see Compendium, p. 32), along with several other opportunities to have forum discussions, forces interaction and decreases the psychological distance so common in online classes.

Teachers who must teach totally online have the challenge of helping students acquire proper speaking opportunities. Students must arrange to tape all of their speeches to send in for evaluation and grading. Clear rules for taping the speech must be included in the course management information. Social interaction opportunities in a totally online class are crucial, and you should seek to support those students who must tape themselves in different situations each time. Students who never meet together can benefit from well-structured forum discussions concerning their varied speaking experiences.

Suggested Readings

The following section contains select references to books, journal articles, online and other resources to help you with specific needs in online course design and development.

Books

Feldman, Robert S., and Christopher Poirier. Distance Learning Integration Guide to Accompany Understanding Psychology. *New York: McGraw-Hill Companies, 2002.*
A step-by step framework for teaching a distance-learning course, this integration guide helps instructors at any level design and teach an introductory course in psychology. It contains an overview of distance learning, a framework for course design, and tips for teaching that transfer easily to other disciplines.

Horton, Sarah. Web Teaching Guide – A Practical Approach to Creating Course Websites. *New Haven: Yale University Press, 2000.*
This is a guide for educators who are in the process of course design and implementation. It shows how a well-designed website can enhance teaching, enrich course content, and provide opportunities for collaboration and customization.

Howard, Diane. Enhanced by Technology, Not Diminished. *New York: McGraw-Hill Primus Custom Publishing, 2003.*
This book provides guidance on how to communicate effectively via websites, e-mail, discussion groups, e-communities, and audio and video conferencing. It also addresses effective e-learning, video streaming, webcasting, e-job hunting and e-publishing from the perspective that we are enhanced, not diminished or replaced, by modern communication technology.

Lynch, Patrick, and Sarah Horton. Web Style Guide – Basic Design Principles for Creating Websites. *2nd ed. New Haven: Yale University Press, 2001.*
This book is written to help instructors publish durable content on the Web, according to solid design principles rather than trendy ones. Its aim is to help readers understand design principles that make content as easy for users to understand as possible.

Moore, Gary S., Dan Lange, and Kathryn Winograd. You Can Teach Online – Building a Creative Learning Environment. *New York: McGraw-Hill, 2001.*
Well illustrated, with easy-to-follow examples of pedagogy and tools useful to faculty in online course development, this book contains links to a course showcase that provides examples of online courses in different disciplines.

Book Chapters

Bonk, Curtis J., and Thomas H. Reynolds. "Learner-Centered Web Instruction for Higher Order Thinking, Teamwork and Apprenticeship." Web-Based Instruction. *Ed. Badrul H. Kahn. Englewood Cliffs, NJ: Educational Technology Publications, 1997. 167-178.*
Contains lists of critical thinking and collaborative learning techniques.

Bonk, Curtis J., et al. "A Ten-Level Web Integration Continuum for Higher Education." Instructional and Cognitive Impacts of Web-Based Education. *Ed. Beverly Abbey. Hershey, USA: Idea Group Publishing, 2000. 56-77*
Contains a detailed continuum of pedagogical choices faculty must consider in developing Web-based course components.

Bonk, Curtis J., Robert A. Wisher, and Ji-Yeon Lee. "Moderating Learner-Centered E-Learning: Problems and Solutions, Benefits and Implications." Asynchronous Learning: Institutional, Pedagogical and Assessment Issues in Higher Education. *Ed. I. Giles and P. Robinson. Stylus Publishing (in press)*
Discusses major issues and trends in online learning, including learner-centered movement, team and collaborative environments, new roles for online instructors, and key benefits and implications of e-learning, as well as associated problems and potential solutions.

Bonk, Curtis J., et al. "Finding the Instructor in Post-Secondary Online Learning: Pedagogical, Social, Managerial and Technological Locations." Teaching and Learning Online: New Pedagogies for New Technologies. *Ed. J. Stephenson. Starling, VA: Kogan Page, 2001*
Contains helpful and practical advice for online instructors in the areas of pedagogy, social interaction, management and technology from a team of authors with extensive online teaching experience.

Book Review

Slabinski, Anthony P. Rev. of Evaluation and Implementation of Distance Learning: Technologies, Tools and Techniques, *by F. Belanger and D. Jordan.* Journal of Instruction Delivery Systems *16.2: 30-33.*
Suggests basic considerations when providing distance learning.

Periodicals

Bonk, Curtis J., and Jack A. Cummings. "A Dozen Recommendations for Placing the Student at the Center of Web-Based Learning." Educational Media International *35.2*

(1998): 82-89.
Explains twelve recommendations for learner-centered instruction based on teaching experiences.

Bonk, Curtis J., and Vanessa Dennen. "Teaching on the Web: With a Little Help from My Pedagogical Friends." Journal of Computing in Higher Education *11.1 (Fall 1999): 3-28.*
Discusses costs and benefits of Web teaching tools, illustrates benefits from learner point of view, explains ways to embed critical and creative thinking, as well as cooperative learning and teamwork, into course design. Sample Web course tools are presented with a review of several types of Web courseware and conferencing systems.

Carlson, Randal D., and Judi Repman. "Activating Web-Based E-Learning." International Journal on E-Learning *(April-June 2002): 7-10.*
Examines resources that incorporate basic principles of active learning into e-learning environments.

Frederick, Patricia. "The Need for Alternative Authentic Assessments in Online Learning Environments." Journal of Instruction Delivery Systems 16.1: 17-20.
Assessing students in an online environment means changing from traditional testing to more student-centered testing as a richer way to foster student learning. Excellent article analyzing the need for valid assessment and evaluation.

Hobbs, Dan L. "A Constructivist Approach to Web Course Design: A Review of the Literature." International Journal on E-Learning *(April-June 2002): 60-65.*
Excellent article for those new to online course development. Discusses design methodologies such as "Learning by Objective"; establishes need for collaborative learning communities; and discusses communication as pedagogy.

Klemm, W. R. "Eight Ways to Get Students More Engaged in Online Conferences." Higher *Education* Journal *26.1: 62-64. 14 November 2000 <http://cvm.tamu.edu/wklemm/Eight%20ways/8waystoengage.htm>.*
Suggests practical tips to get students to talk meaningfully with each other online.

MacKinnon, Gregory R. "Practical Advice for First-Time Online Instructors: A Qualitative Study." Journal of Instruction Delivery Systems *16.1: 21-25.*
Contains experiences of first-time online instructors and resultant recommendations for preparation, course structure, communication , assignments and assessment.

Murray, Bridget. "Reinventing Class Discussion Online." Monitor on Psychology *4 (April 2000): 54-56.*
Techniques are discussed for getting students to talk meaningfully on the Web, as well as an extensive list of pitfalls to avoid in Web discussion assignments.

Shuey, Sharon. "Assessing Online Learning in Higher Education." Journal of Instruction Delivery Systems *16.2: 13-18.*
Discusses how to build assessment techniques into an online course.

Silvester, John M. *"Bring 'Community' into the Online Learning Environment: What, Why and How."* Journal of Instruction Delivery Systems *15.4: 17-21.*
Helps instructors to facilitate community online by defining community, explaining why it is important to learning and how it can best be created online. Contains documented best practices from experts.

Sorensen, Elsebeth Korsgaard, and Eugene S. Takle. *"Collaborative Knowledge Building in Web-Based Learning: Assessing the Quality of Dialogue."* International Journal on E-Learning *(January-March 2002): 28-32.*
How to structure and grade reflective student dialogue.

Wakley, Del. *"The New Rules of Engagement: Keeping Online Students Involved and On Track in Asynchronous Discussion Forums."* Journal of Instruction Delivery Systems *16.2: 6-12.*
Contains models for online socialization, kinds of discussion, rules for discussion and techniques for maintaining student interest, participation and satisfaction.

Vranesh, Richard H., *"Recommendations for the Use of Collaborative Learning Tools to Accommodate Divergent Student Learning Styles."* Journal of Instruction Delivery Systems *16.1: 10-14.*
Although based on scientific inquiry, this article contains interesting descriptions of student learning styles and what types of assignments appeal to each.

Online Sources

Arsham, Hossien. *"Interactive Education: Impact of the Internet on Learning and Teaching." 5 November 2002 <http://ubmail.ubalt.edu/~harsham/interactive.htm>.*
How to begin, operate and make Wed-based courses successful and enjoyable. An instructor documents his experiences.

"ADEC Guiding Principles for Distance Teaching and Learning." 2 Feb. 2003 <http://www.adec.edu/admin/papers/distance-learning_principles.html>.
Contains guidelines for creating distance-learning assignments from the American Distance Education Consortium.

Florida Gulf Coast University Faculty Development and Support *website. 2000 <http://www.fgcu.edu/onlinedesign/intro.html>.*
Contains detailed information for instructors who are developing online courses.

Multimedia Educational Resource for Learning Online and Training. 18 Apr. 2003. <http://www.merlot.org>.
Fantastic collection of articles on distance education in most disciplines. Communication is not included at the time this book was published. Excellent articles available in the categories of Teaching and Learning in Higher Education.

Multimedia: Educational Resource for Leaning Online and Training *"Teaching at an Internet Distance: The Pedagogy of Online Teaching and Learning: The Report of a 1998-99 University of Illinois Faculty Seminar." 7 December 1999. <http://www.merlot.org>.*
  Strongly suggested as required reading to directors and administrators, as well as teachers. Discusses status of online instruction at the University of Illinois, adverse faculty reaction, political issues, overview of online teaching and learning, evaluation, conclusions and recommendations for online program at UI.

Permissions Form

This manual discusses using exercises from *The Art of Public Speaking* for your online public speaking course. If you choose to use additional sources for your online public speaking course and include them on your website (rather than simply linking to another website), be aware that you may need to obtain permission to use them. The guidelines for when you do and do not need to obtain permission to use a source are beyond the scope of this book. However, in general, when considering whether or not you need to obtain permission, think of your online course website as though it were a printed text. If you would have to obtain permission to use the materials in a print publication, then you would need to obtain permission to use them online.

The following document is a form letter you can adapt and use should you need to obtain permissions:

Date
Manager
Permissions Department
Publisher

Dear Sir/Madam:

_____ is preparing for publication the
following work:

Title:
Author:
Estimated Publication Date:
Formats:
Print Run:
Ancillaries:

We request your permission to (adapt and) include the following material in this and all
subsequent editions of the book, including versions made by nonprofit organizations for
use by blind or physically handicapped persons (and in all foreign language translations
and other derivative works) for distribution (throughout the world/in North America):

Author(s) and/or editor(s):
Title:
Copyright Date:
Exact Material: figure _____on p. _____ (see attached copy)
                or
                excerpt on pp. _____ (see attached copy)

Please indicate agreement by signing and returning the enclosed copy of this letter. In
signing, you warrant that you are the sole owner of the rights granted and that your
material does not infringe upon the copyright or other rights of anyone. If you do not
control these rights in their entirety, we would appreciate your letting us know to whom
we should apply.

Thank you for your assistance.
Sincerely,

AGREED TO AND ACCEPTED:

By
  Name: _____ Date: _____

  Title: _____

References

"ADEC Guiding Principles for Distance Teaching and Learning."
<http://www.adec.edu/admin/papers/distance-learning_principles.html>.

Bonk, Curtis J., and Thomas H. Reynolds. "Learner-Centered Web Instruction for Higher
Order Thinking, Teamwork and Apprenticeship." Web-Based Instruction. *Ed. Badrul*
H. Kahn. Englewood Cliffs, NJ: Educational Technology Publications, 1997. 167-
178.

Bonk, Curtis J., and Vanessa Dennen. "Teaching on the Web: With a Little Help from My
Pedagogical Friends." Journal of Computing in Higher Education *11.1 (Fall 1999):*
3-28.

Bonk, Curtis J. "Mediating Discussion and Mentoring Students for Interactive Online
Learning." Workshop. Indiana University-Purdue University at Indianapolis. 1999.

Carlson, Randal D., and Judi Repman. "Activating Web-Based E-Learning."
International Journal on E-Learning *(April-June 2002): 7-10.*

Cochrane, Jennifer, Kathy Fox and Kate Thedwall. The R110 Student Coursebook, *6 ed.*
to accompany The Art of Public Speaking, *7 ed. New York: McGraw-Hill, 2002.*

Hobbs, Dan L. "A Constructivist Approach to Web Course Design: A Review of the
Literature." International Journal on E-Learning *(April-June 2002): 60-65.*

Horton, Sarah. Web Teaching Guide – A Practical Approach to Creating Course
Websites. *New Haven: Yale University Press, 2000.*

Lynch, Patrick, and Sarah Horton. Web Style Guide – Basic Design Principles for
Creating Websites. *2nd ed. New Haven: Yale University Press, 2001.*

Shuey, Sharon. "Assessing Online Learning in Higher Education." Journal of Instruction
Delivery Systems *16. 2: 13-18.*

Wakley, Del. "The New Rules of Engagement: Keeping Online Students Involved and On
Track in Asynchronous Discussion Forums." Journal of Instruction Delivery Systems
16.2: 6-12.

Glossary

Active learning: Meaningful interaction between the learner and the instructional content and/or instructional process. It is characterized by the student as "initiator" of learning. (See passive learning.)

ADEC: American Distance Learning Consortium (http:www.adec.edu).

Adjunct: A Web course in which the Web is used as an informational, supportive delivery system only, and the method of instruction takes place off-line either in class, by voice mail, by instructional tapes, etc.

Assignment Design Characteristics: Guidelines for effective Web learning exercises.

Asynchronous: Not occurring at the same time." Refers to the delayed nature of informational transfer over the Web. Not real time.

Chat: Real-time or synchronous informational transfer on the Web. Chat functionality is generally a feature of most courseware.

Collaborative learning: Learning that can be done in groups or partnerships.

Computer-Mediated Instruction (CMI): Teaching and learning that occurs via the Internet.

Course Design Principle: A guideline that connects the characteristics of the Web to course design.

Course management information: Information that organizes a Web-based course. It generally contains everything except the schedule and assignments, and is sometimes referred to as "housekeeping" information.

Courseware: Type of information management software (Web CT, Blackboard, Oncourse, Angel, PageOut, etc.) used for online courses.

Discussion forum/board: Feature of courseware that allows asynchronous public postings to take place.

Distance learning: Refers to learning done remotely and not in a traditional classroom, such as Internet courses, correspondence courses, etc.

E-learning: Learning done via a computer (CMI). Also known as Web learning or online learning.

Electronic café: An area created for discussion or chat, usually for socialization.

Flaming: Negative, inflammatory electronic messaging, sometimes designed to influence opinion.

Interactive websites: Websites that provide opportunities for students to act and react with the content and process of the site; features a give and take of information.

Internet: A global connection of interlinked computer networks.

Learner centered: A type of learning or learning environment that places the responsibility for learning directly on the student, rather than the teacher.

Learning environment: Area on the Web that is managed for teaching and learning.

Learning platform: See *courseware*.

Learning style: A person's preferred way of perceiving and processing information (e.g. structured vs. unstructured environment, hands-on experimentation vs. reflective observance, auditory, visual, etc.).

Lurking: Observing the interactions of others in online chat or discussions without participating.

Mixed-mode: A type of web course in which there is computer mediated delivery of content and instruction, and face-to-face delivery of most or all speeches.

Netiquette: Rules for communicating via e-mail and other forms of online messaging.

Offline: Using the computer, but not connected to the Internet.

Online: Connected to the Internet.

Online Learning Center (OLC): Area of http://www.mhhe.com/lucas8 that contains chapter-by-chapter objectives and a variety of ancillary materials for *The Art of Public Speaking,* including the Top 100 American Speeches of the 20th Century.

PageOut: A template created by McGraw-Hill that allows instructors to create their own personal websites.

Passive learning: Learning by informational transfer from teacher to student. It is characterized by the student as "receiver" of information and the teacher as "source."

PowerWeb: Part of the Online Learning Center containing the following features: articles with assessments; news feeds and weekly updates; Web research and study tips for students; course-related links and interactive exercises; instructor resource guide and links to news articles by topic. Access to PowerWeb is included when you adopt *The Art of Public Speaking,* 8th ed.

Synchronous: Occurring at the same time or in real time.

Threaded discussion: Public postings in a forum platform where individuals have a written discussion on a topic or issue by making multiple comments on the remarks of others.

Web based: Residing on the Web.

Webcast: Video broadcasts via the Internet.

World Wide Web: A hypertext information system that allows users to access materials from the Internet. Frequently referred to simply as the Web.